TEACHING ON THE EDUCATION FRONTIER

TEACHING ON THE EDUCATION FRONTIER

Instructional Strategies for Online and Blended Classrooms

Grades 5–12

Kristin Kipp

Foreword by Susan Patrick

JB JOSSEY-BASS™
A Wiley Brand

Published by Jossey-Bass
A Wiley Brand
One Montgomery Street, Suite 1200, San Francisco, CA 94104-4594—www.josseybass.com

Library of Congress Cataloging-in-Publication Data has been applied for and is on file with the Library of Congress.

ISBN 978-1-118-44977-6 (paper); ISBN 978-1-118-64652-6 (ebk.); ISBN 978-1-118-64660-1 (ebk.); ISBN 978-1-118-64671-7 (ebk.)

Printed in the United States of America
FIRST EDITION
PB Printing 10 9 8 7 6 5 4 3 2 1

CONTENTS

For my husband, Dan,
my harshest critic but also my greatest supporter

ABOUT THIS BOOK

This book provides best practices for online teachers. It is filled with strategies that I have used in my own online classroom with success as well as insights and tips from online teachers throughout the field. It will help you to set up your online classroom, design assignments, communicate with students, manage the workload, and much more. The chapters are designed to stand alone so you may read them in any order. Feel free to flip immediately to the topic that most interests you! Teachers new to online teaching may want to begin with chapters 1 through 4 for basic ideas around course philosophy, structure, and relationships. More experienced online teachers will find more advanced strategies in chapters 5 through 13. Although blended (also known as *hybrid*) teaching strategies are woven throughout the text through special ''focus on blended learning'' features, chapter 14 is specifically focused on blended learning and finding ways to use digital tools to supplement and extend the traditional classroom. The following summarizes each of the chapters in the text to help you to find the topics you're most interested in.

Chapter 1: The Many Variables of Online and Blended Teaching

This chapter considers the numerous variables inherent in online learning programs, such as whether a program is self-paced or a cohort model, whether the program has its own curriculum or a purchased curriculum, whether the students are full-time online or part-time online, and so on. Each of these variables complicates the teaching situation and affects the way that teachers present their courses on a day-by-day and week-by-week basis. This chapter explores those variables and considers instructional strategies for coping with various teaching situations.

Chapter 2: Course Philosophy

This chapter explores a basic philosophy for what makes a good online course. It operates on the premise that any good online course will have three fundamental elements: first, that students will connect to the content; second, that students will connect with each other; finally, that students will connect with the teacher. If any one of the three elements is missing, student engagement and therefore learning will suffer. The ideas in this chapter provide the teaching and learning framework for the rest of the strategies in the text.

Chapter 3: Preparing to Teach an Online Course

This chapter considers all the decisions that have to be made as you begin to set up your basic course structure. It provides recommendations for elements such as the syllabus, the course organization, pacing, and accessing student data. If the course is not organized thoughtfully from the beginning, it is doomed before it ever begins.

Chapter 4: Building Relationships with Students

This chapter considers ways to build relationships with students whom you've never met face-to-face. Through student stories and case studies, it explores ways to connect with kids and encourage them to share their stories with you. Without those connections, students are unmotivated to do their best in the online course.

Chapter 5: Using Announcements Effectively

This chapter considers how to use the announcements feature of the learning management system (LMS) to engage students as well as keep them moving in the right direction. It will also consider how to use those announcements to keep the course interesting and, at times, even funny! Also included will be options for how to include your voice in the course announcements through podcasts and vodcasts.

Chapter 6: Discussion Board Strategies and Facilitation

This chapter considers how to facilitate a discussion board. This can be one of the most daunting tasks of moving into an online or blended classroom because it's so different from the way we lead discussions face-to-face. This chapter provides recommendations on how much to be involved in the discussion and how to deepen the learning with quality posts and prompts. It also provides some tips for having students facilitate discussions.

Chapter 7: Teaching Synchronous Sessions

This chapter provides an introduction to teaching synchronous sessions or webinars. It provides an overview of what's possible in a webinar and focuses on how to move from lecture-style webinars into something that's more interactive and engaging. It also considers what the proper role is for synchronous sessions in online learning and what makes them most effective.

Chapter 8: Creating and Modifying Assignments

This chapter is aimed at teachers who have author or editor privileges in the content management system. It considers how to create engaging assignments that value critical thinking and originality. It also explains a process for looking at existing course content and deciding how to modify that content to best meet student needs.

Chapter 9: Collaborating in Online Courses

This chapter focuses on the third part of the course philosophy from chapter 3 — connecting students with each other. It explores ways to use blogs, wikis, groups, and other course tools to have students working together to deepen their learning. Lots of concrete examples are included.

Chapter 10: Differentiating Assignments

This chapter explains how the online course environment can help to customize student learning. Thinking about designing thirty different learning paths for students can be overwhelming. This chapter introduces strategies to differentiate in a practical way that won't significantly increase the teacher's workload.

Chapter 11: Grading and Feedback

This chapter considers how to provide in-depth, meaningful feedback to students. It focuses on what types of feedback make a difference in student achievement and how to provide that feedback in an efficient way.

Chapter 12: Accessibility, Communication, and Office Hours

This chapter focuses on how to make yourself available as an instructor in an online class. It explores ideas such as office hours and tutoring as ways to help students understand that they are never alone and always have their teacher's support. It also discusses communication strategies via e-mail, text messaging, and phone so that students are in constant communication with the teacher.

Chapter 13: Time Management and Routines

This chapter considers how to achieve a positive work-life balance while working from home or on a flexible schedule. Basic weekly work flows and to-do lists are shared along with practical time management tips.

Chapter 14: Strategies for Blended Learning

Although any of the strategies in this text can be applied to blended learning situations, this chapter specifically focuses on how to organize a blended learning classroom. It provides criteria for deciding when a task is best completed online and when it is best completed face-to-face. It also provides some examples of blended assignments: assignments or projects in which a portion of the work is completed face-to-face and a portion is completed online.

Chapter 15: Training to Teach Online

This chapter considers various routes to teaching online and which paths are most effective for quickly learning the skills of an online facilitator. Specific resources (websites, books, blogs, and courses) are recommended.

At the end of the book I've also provided information on some of the most helpful resources out there for online teaching and learning, including blogs, wikis, and Twitter accounts that online teachers should consider following.

Teaching in the education frontier can be daunting; however, it's also incredibly fulfilling. This is a rewarding journey. Turn the page and let's begin!

ABOUT THE AUTHOR

KRISTIN KIPP is a full-time online English teacher and instructional coach for Jeffco's Virtual Academy in Golden, Colorado. She was named the 2011 National Online Teacher of the Year by the International Association for K–12 Online Learning (iNACOL) and the Southern Regional Education Board (SREB). In the past she has taught eighth through twelfth grades, both virtually and in a face-to-face classroom. She presents across the country about best practices in online learning and blogs at http://www.educationfrontier.org. She lives in Evergreen, Colorado with her husband and three children.

FOREWORD

Ours is a world of high-tech, high-touch learning. This shift to a digital world and an increasingly knowledge-oriented society is influencing the way students and teachers interact with environments around them, how they connect with peers and experts, how they access news and information, and how they research, write, and communicate. The flexibility for students to learn from the best teachers possible in highly personalized environments, allowing them to engage with dynamic, adaptive curriculum any time, everywhere, is a reality for a growing number of young people around the globe. The same flexibility and personalization is transforming the role of the teacher and freeing time to design, implement, and adapt curriculum to work with students one-on-one, on a lesson-by-lesson basis.

Just as education must not be designed as a one-size-fits-all solution for students, teaching in a variety of online and blended learning environments is not a monolithic endeavor and requires varied approaches, strategies, and pedagogies. It is this art of teaching using online and blended learning tools and twenty-first-century strategies that is explained so clearly in this book.

Meeting every student's unique needs is important if learners are to stay on their own leading edge of learning—maximizing engagement and potential and targeting student agency based on interests and passions. Whether students are in a physical classroom guided by teachers personalizing instruction using digital content and resources or students are taking one or more classes completely online, each pedagogical approach requires reflection and integration of emerging methods of mentoring, modeling, instructing, supporting, tutoring, assessing, evaluating, and coaching kids in new learning environments.

Learning has changed dramatically in a relatively short period of time—from using a single textbook to having myriad resources at the fingertips of teachers and their students online, in apps, and through digital books. Online courses and immediate access to journals and original source materials signify the powerful shift from twentieth- to twenty-first-century tools and technologies in the learning process. A knowledge economy demands that students work in teams, problem solve, and communicate differently, and the world of online and blended learning opens up the vast potential for highly personalized, student-centered learning options that provide all with access to world-class educational opportunities.

Even as there is a great shift occurring in the education space, the corner-stone of the overall success for new models of learning, as it turns out, remains the same in online and blended learning environments as it does in traditional classes—excellent teachers who are the driving force and the gold standard for high-quality learning. Understanding the evolving roles of educators as multi-faceted professionals, armed with tools for personalization, data-driven individualized instruction, and new methodologies to bring collaboration and communication into the twenty-first century is critical if we are to advance learning in the game-changing ways kids need to be successful in the modern world and workplace.

Whether in real-time, synchronous models, or flexible asynchronous learning environments, knowing and mapping each student's learning goals, performance, skills, and disposition is critical for effective instruction in new learning models.

The transition from traditional classroom teacher to leading an online or blended course comes with a learning curve attached. Teaching is not an easy profession in either case but many find that the tools available in a technology-driven learning environment are exactly what they need in order to bring them back to that original impulse to teach—one-on-one engagement with all students individually to bring them forward in their education through personalized instruction. This is an instructional model that breaks the one-size-fits-all approach to education, freeing students to go further and deeper in building knowledge and identifying the best path toward achievement and mastery of essential content, skills, and dispositions.

I can't tell you how many online and blended teachers have shared with me the sheer joy they felt at the moment they moved beyond the notion of a disconnected classroom and began to realize the power of a learning environment in which they were free to abandon "teaching to the middle" and truly work with each of their students as individuals. Those very same teachers gladly share that though they may not be in the same physical space as their students, they are able to develop stronger bonds with them than they were ever able to in a traditional classroom.

Kristin Kipp was a recipient of the SREB/iNACOL National Online Teacher of the Year award, and her commitment to excellence and to personalized learning for all teachers and students is highlighted throughout each and every section of this book. From the fundamentals of communication to the art of differentiating assignments, this guide provides a road map for new teachers, a refresher for more experienced ones, and a primer for those interested in exploring the role of teachers in the dynamic, new education models using online and blended learning emerging today.

Susan Patrick
President and CEO, International
Association for K–12 Online Learning

INTRODUCTION

In fall 2007 I had just begun my fifth year of teaching in a face-to-face classroom. I was teaching freshman and sophomore English in a very high-performing high school. Although I truly enjoyed my job, I was feeling an itch to try something new. I wanted to find some new ways to engage kids and take their learning deeper but I wasn't sure exactly what that looked like. When I heard about the benefits of a virtual classroom, I wanted to try it out. That was the year I wrote my first online course and began to explore what online teaching and learning was all about.

Perhaps that's where you are in your journey. You're just beginning to enter the education frontier. You want to try some new techniques for teaching online or in a blended classroom. You want to know what good online courses look like and what a good teacher should do in an online space. Or perhaps you've already taught one or more online or blended classes but you feel like you want to know how to make them more effective or engaging. This book is meant to be your guide. Its purpose is to provide an introduction to online teaching for those who are just beginning their journey as well as new strategies for experienced online teachers. I hope to help you avoid some of the pitfalls I fell into so that you can thrive as an online teacher from day one.

Online education is a significant disruption in the education field. The *Speak Up* report by Project Tomorrow estimates that three times as many high school students and twice as many middle school students had access to online courses in 2011 compared to 2007. By 2020, it's projected that 50 percent of all high school courses will be taught online (Christensen, Horn, & Johnson, 2009). This is a field that is growing by leaps and bounds. More and more school districts are beginning to see the value of online education for students, and online education is filling a void left in the education sector as a whole. It's providing flexible options for students and helping turn high school dropouts into high school graduates. It's important work.

At the same time, there is a lot of criticism of online education. In 2011, the *New York Times* and the Associated Press published multiple articles questioning the quality of online programs. They questioned whether it was too easy for students to cheat in these programs. They questioned whether online high schools are simply degree mills (Gabriel, 2011). They even questioned whether the numerous online learning corporations are simply interested in making a profit rather than serving students (Saul, 2011; Wyatt & Moreno, 2011). These are valid questions that we as an industry have to address. Now that online learning has become an option for so many students across the country, the question becomes, ''How do we improve the quality of online education so that it's not just available for all students but actually improves student achievement?''

Even with the media criticism of online education, there are also signs of progress and high-quality results in online classrooms. A 2010 meta-analysis by SRI International for the US Department of Education showed that students who were learning online performed better than students in face-to-face classrooms. In fact, students who learned at least partially online scored in the 59th percentile on standardized tests as compared to the 50th percentile for students who learned solely in face-to-face classrooms (US Department of Education, 2010). There is definitely promise. The question we must address is, ''How do we make that promise a reality?''

Online education is a young field. There are many issues we need to address in order to realize our potential. What does quality look like in an online classroom and how do we achieve it? I tend to agree with Susan Patrick, CEO of the iNACOL, who says that ''teachers will remain the gold standard of quality in every class'' (Patrick, personal e-mail). When teachers are intimately involved in an online course and in working with online students on a regular basis, quality will result. Great teaching leads to high-quality learning, whether the teacher is online or face-to-face.

TEACHING ON THE EDUCATION FRONTIER

CHAPTER ONE

THE MANY VARIABLES OF ONLINE AND BLENDED TEACHING

ESSENTIAL QUESTIONS:

- What variables should you consider in your teaching situation?
- How might your teaching situation affect the methods you can or cannot use in your online classroom?
- What factors should you consider when looking at a new job and how does the school's teaching model line up with your teaching philosophy?
- How can you overcome challenges in your teaching situation?
- Which of the following variables do you prefer and why?
  - Self-paced versus cohort approach
  - Full-time versus part-time online students
  - Blended versus fully online courses
  - Create-your-own versus purchased curriculum
  - Teacher as course author and organizer versus teacher as facilitator only
  - Teacher evaluation based on course completion versus traditional evaluation systems

One of the most exciting (and terrifying!) parts of going into online education is that there is so much variety in the types of programs out there. Seemingly hundreds of variables have to be considered in any given teaching situation. Are the students full-time or part-time online students? Will the course work be fully online or will there be some face-to-face component? Will I be writing the course or is the course already created? Do I have permissions to change the course for each group of students I work with? Although you may not always have control over all these variables, it's important to consider the impact they have on the teaching experience and, if a situation is not ideal, think about how you might modify your methods to make the best of it. Consider the following situations. What might the teaching experience be like in each of these?

Situation one: School A is a full-time virtual school. It's a program that is led by a school district. All courses are created by the district's curriculum team and, although online teachers can modify the order of the content, they cannot edit the content itself. All students are full-time online students who are working from their homes. Teachers work under a standard teacher contract, which means that they can never have more than 170 students (secondary) or 40 students (elementary) at one time. The school runs on a traditional semester schedule so students pace together through the course as a cohort.

Situation two: School B is a full-time virtual school run by a for-profit corporation. The school takes students on a rolling enrollment basis so all the students are at different parts of the course at different times. Course content is created by the company so teachers do not have editing privileges in their courses. However, the course content is run through a social networking site built just for the organization so teachers can build a custom class website including announcements, discussion boards, status updates, and so on. Teachers tend to have heavier class loads because they do no course creation work. Most teachers have around 250 students at a time.

Situation three: School C is a state-run virtual school. All students are part-time in the online school and part-time in a brick-and-mortar school. Teachers work part-time, usually moonlighting after working in a traditional school during the day. Courses are created fully by the teacher before the start of the semester and teachers maintain editing privileges for all course content. Because teachers are moonlighting, they generally don't have course loads of more than twenty students at a time. Students generally work as a cohort but the school takes late enrollments, up to six weeks after the start of the course. Therefore, there are always groups of students who are not with the rest of class. Teachers are paid on a per-student basis for any student who passes the course.

As you can see, the variety in these situations is enormous and thus the teaching strategies would have to be modified to be successful in each of these cases. The Innosight Institute, in their report *The Rise of K–12 Blended Learning* (Horn & Staker, 2011), identified additional variables in blended learning including whether or not students meet face-to-face and how often, how much teaching teachers are doing or if they are involved more as a support, whether or not there are **synchronous** components to the course (elements that are happening at the same time), and even whether the course is taught in a computer lab or if students are primarily at home. As professional educators, it is our responsibility to make the best of each teaching situation. Let's consider some of these many variables and how they affect the teacher's role in the learning environment.

SELF-PACED VERSUS COHORT APPROACH

One of the many benefits of online learning is the opportunity for students to have customized learning. In a self-paced approach, everyone is working on different parts of a course at different times. So, Johnny, who has a learning disability, might take nine months to complete a semester-long course whereas Jennifer, who is an advanced student, completes the course in two months. As Susan Patrick, president of iNACOL, says for a learning situation like this, ''Learning is the constant and time is the variable'' (personal e-mail). Florida Virtual School and K12, Inc., are prominent examples of programs that use this model. There are huge benefits to this approach for students who are motivated and can work through the course as their time permits. They can take as much or as little time as needed to learn the course material. However, there are also some challenges involved. If students are not motivated, they may never finish a particular course. They still need a lot of communication with their instructor so that they are motivated to continue. Also, it's difficult to create a sense of community in a course like this because students are rarely on the same content at the same time. As a teacher, you have to be creative about bringing the students together occasionally for those shared learning experiences that are so important to cognitive development.

The alternative to a self-paced approach would be a cohort-based system. Students pace together through a class over the course of a traditional semester, much like a traditional classroom. The teacher assigns due dates to each section of the course and communicates those to students. Synchronous sessions can be developed based on topics that the students are working on at the same time. Classroom discussions and group projects are a regular part of the course content because the course is a shared experience with a shared timeline. On the down side, the course is less likely to be customized to a student's needs and it's less flexible overall. Although students do have flexibility within some parts of the course (the flexibility of doing their work on the weekend instead of Monday through Friday, for example), for the most part they are limited by a course calendar and due dates. Those due dates can be motivating for students who need deadlines or those who procrastinate. However, the due dates can also be discouraging for students who fall behind or just need more time to complete the course work.

Quality teaching can occur in either of these learning options. Usually the course parameters are set by the school and the teaching program. It's important for administrators to be clear about which model they will be using and how teachers can facilitate within that model.

Keys to Success in a Self-Paced Model

For teachers who are working in a self-paced model, it's crucial to pay attention to developing a classroom community even though your students are working on different content at different times. The classroom community and classroom culture are very motivating for students and can be an important part of the learning experience. That might mean that you maintain a "cyber cafe" within your course discussion board where students can chat about off-topic ideas whenever they would like, much as they would between classes in a traditional school. You could also create group projects that students can contribute to as they get to them, such as a wiki that students are adding to as a culminating project on a particular unit. Discussion boards can also be a vital part of the class but they may need to be on more general topics or set up so that students can add to them at flexible times. Refer to chapter 6 for more ideas on how to facilitate these vital elements in your classroom.

Keys to Success in a Cohort-Based Model

In a cohort-based model, it's important to give students flexibility within the structure. Publish your due dates as soon as possible and communicate them to students in several different ways. They should be within the announcements, on a course calendar, in the syllabus, and also sent via e-mail. Just as in face-to-face classrooms where students need everything repeated five times, your online students will benefit from repetition. You'll also need to consider whether or not to charge a late penalty if students don't meet their deadlines and consider how long you will accept late work from a particular unit. These are personal decisions that will depend on your teaching philosophy. The most important thing is that you've clearly communicated those expectations within your course syllabus and you share the rationale with students.

FULL-TIME VERSUS PART-TIME ONLINE STUDENTS

Students who come to online programs do so for a variety of reasons. Some just like computers and want to do more of their work via technology. Others have things going on in their personal lives and need the flexibility of online learning in order to continue their education while working full-time, dealing with an illness, taking care of an infant, pursuing a professional sport, and so on. It's difficult to make generalizations about such a huge variety of needs. However, there are some trends within enrollments that can affect student achievement.

Students who are enrolled full-time in an online school are generally there because something in their traditional schooling wasn't working. Full-time online students tend to be classified as more ''at-risk'' than their traditional school counterparts. In some cases, they've checked out of the school process and are using online school as a final effort to avoid dropping out. These students tend to have lower course completion percentages and tend to be behind on their credits to graduate on time.

Students who are enrolled part-time in an online school are usually looking for something that's lacking in their traditional school. They may want more flexibility or they may want a course that's not offered locally. Unlike full-time online students, they haven't checked out of a traditional model. They still attend a regular brick-and-mortar school for at least one or two classes per day. They're still in the routine of school. They just added online courses for additional challenge or to meet a certain need. The Innosight Institute labels this a ''self-blend'' model of online education, in which students choose which courses to take online and which to take face-to-face based on what better meets their needs (Horn & Staker, 2011).

Keys to Success with Full-Time Online Students

For full-time online students, time management is crucial. They are most often working from their homes. There is no bell schedule and they can get distracted by posting updates on a social network, having lunch, getting texts from friends, and so on. Full-time online students benefit greatly from having a teacher or counselor work with them on time management and goal setting. When students first come to full-time online learning, they may be overwhelmed and have no idea where to start. The idea that you could spend an hour and a half on math and just twenty minutes on English in a particular day is foreign to them and it will take some time to adjust.

Full-time online students also benefit from proactive communication from their teacher. They need to feel like they're not alone. E-mails, text messages, instant messaging (IM), and even phone calls should be a regular part of their course so that they don't feel isolated and they know there's a caring adult who is there to help at any time. They won't always reach out for help so it's important that you're making the first step as their teacher to let them know that you care about them and you're there for them.

Keys to Success with Part-Time Online Students

Although part-time online students are still in the swing of regular school and tend to be more successful in online courses, they also tend to be overscheduled. I once worked with a part-time online student who attended a face-to-face school six hours a day, worked twenty hours a week, and starred in the school play. Then he wondered why he just could never seem to keep up on his online courses! For these students, it's important to communicate your expectations. Let kids know exactly how long they should plan to work in the course each week and hold them accountable for deadlines. However, also be ready to help them catch up when they inevitably fall behind because they simply have too much going on in their lives. Balancing a workload is a very grown-up skill and it's important to help them develop it early.

Whether you have full-time online students, part-time online students, or a blend of both will depend on your program's model. Any of these students can be successful in online learning as long as they have support that's tailored to their needs. Early in the semester, it's important to survey your students so you know what their needs might be. A question as simple as, "Is there anything going on in your life that might affect your school performance?" can reveal a lot about your student's needs and how you can help them be successful.

BLENDED VERSUS FULLY ONLINE COURSES

In recent years, blended learning has absolutely exploded onto the online learning scene. Basically, **blended (or hybrid) learning** seeks to combine elements of face-to-face instruction with elements of online instruction. Students are being given all sorts of options. They can take courses fully online, they can take courses fully face-to-face with some sort of online enrichment, or they can take courses that are a blend of both. Blended courses can have a variety of schedules. Some meet one day a week face-to-face with the rest of the week online. Others meet every other day or only once a month.

As a teaching professional, it's important to understand fully the model that you're working under and begin to think about how to emphasize that model's

Table 1.1 Strengths of Online versus Face-to-Face Teaching

Online Strengths	Face-to-Face Strengths
• Tasks that require multiple sessions	• Complicated, multistep demonstrations
• Tasks that need **web 2.0 tools** (tools students can use on the Internet to create and share content)	• Student presentations requiring a live audience
• Lectures and videos (because they can be paused as needed)	• Organization tasks that require class input
• Tasks in which time may vary among students	• Taking tests and assessments

strengths. For example, in an online lab model in which students work on their courses at least partially in a school computer lab, I know that my students will have the support of a paraprofessional face-to-face at least some of the time they're working on my course. It would be absolutely vital to develop a relationship with that person and communicate with him or her on a regular basis so that students are not getting mixed messages between me, as their teacher, and their paraprofessional, as their supervisor. For more information about blended learning models see chapter 14.

Keys to Success in a Blended Learning Environment

Teachers who are teaching in a blended learning environment truly have the best of both worlds but only if both models and modes of teaching are used thoughtfully. Certain topics and activities are best suited to face-to-face learning, whereas others are best suited to online. The trick is to know the difference. Table 1.1 gives some examples but more information is provided in chapter 14.

Keys to Success in a Fully Online Course

Fully online courses carry with them their own special set of challenges. First, you know that you'll never see your students face-to-face and you'll need to make a special effort to build a relationship with them. It's really important to personalize the course and share pictures with the students so they feel like they know you. You'll also want to provide a space for them to share pictures of themselves and to share their stories. Second, you'll find that some concepts simply must be demonstrated visually in order to be understood, especially in science and math courses. Videos, screencasts, and **vodcasts** (video versions of a podcast) will be an essential part of the course. You can even experiment with creating your own videos to share ideas. It's important to realize how different a fully online course is from a blended or traditional option.

CREATE-YOUR-OWN VERSUS A PURCHASED CURRICULUM

Curriculum is hands-down one of the most challenging aspects to starting an online program. It is a monumental task to create or obtain all of the core courses and electives needed to start a comprehensive high school, much less a whole K–12 program. Many organizations are forced to purchase curriculum in the beginning in order to start a school quickly. There are some wonderful curriculum providers out there. Many have beautiful, interactive content that is engaging to students. However, the quality of the curriculum varies widely. You may find a course that looks beautiful but, on further analysis, turns out to be simply a textbook and a series of quizzes without any interactive projects or assessments that require critical thinking. Curriculum committees need to consider their overall budget as well as their needs when trying to decide on a quality online learning curriculum because some of the best courses also tend to be the most expensive.

However, some schools decide to bypass the purchase process altogether and create their own curriculum from scratch. This can be a great option for large programs with plenty of resources to pull from. Courses can be created that align perfectly with the school's curriculum guides. Every course can follow a similar model and provide a consistent feel for students. Also, because courses are created in the same learning management system where they will be taught, there are usually far fewer technical issues with the course. (Your **learning management system [LMS]** is the space where you teach your online course. It will have basic tools such as a discussion board, grade book, and a place to share content.) Unfortunately, this is a labor-intensive process. Each course needs a content specialist working very closely with an online learning specialist or IT professional who can help translate the content into an interactive, high-quality course. Even then, the process requires significant oversight.

Teachers don't generally get to share in the decision of whether or not to purchase curriculum. Instead, they are handed a course and asked to modify it for the needs of their students. Consider the following as you look at your courses for the first time and decide how to teach them.

Standards in an Online Classroom

All online courses should clearly align to Common Core State Standards as well as the state standards for the state where a course is being taught. Good curriculum developers will be able to share an alignment with you that clearly indicates which standards are addressed in which lessons. An even stronger method is when the standards are identified in the introduction to each session or lesson in student-friendly language so students can clearly see the goal of the instruction.

Keys to Success with Purchased Curriculum

As mentioned previously, purchased curriculum can vary widely in quality. The most common problem is that the courses are built for use in any model (brick-and-mortar, blended, or completely online). Thus, they rarely include discussions or group projects because those would not fit well in a self-paced model. They also tend to over-rely on autograded quizzes because not all programs will have a teacher intimately involved in assessment and grading. When you first receive a prebuilt course that was purchased from another program, it's important to go through all of the content in detail. You should know the course intimately. Consider the following checklist as you evaluate the preexisting assignments:

- Does each unit include student choice?

- Is the course content well-aligned to your district, state, and national standards?

- Does the course value student-to-student interaction?

- Does the course rely too heavily on quizzes? Where can authentic assessments be included?

- Does the course progress from one skill to another in a way that makes logical sense?

- Is the course visually appealing? Are there images and graphics to support visual learners? Are there videos and **podcasts** (audio broadcasts that can be downloaded to media players to support audio learners)? Are there hands-on activities to support kinesthetic learners?

You may also want to evaluate the course using the iNACOL National Standards for Quality Online Courses. They can be a helpful lens. The complete list of the iNACOL National Standards for Quality Online Courses is included in appendix A.

Then, from there, it will be up to you to decide on your priorities. Don't feel like you need to fix the entire course the first time you teach it! However, set a few goals for each unit. For example, you might decide that you want to add more interactive projects and discussions to the prebuilt course. Then you can keep the basic course shell and modify just a few assignments or quizzes in each session to make the course better. After teaching the course for a few years, you'll be amazed to see how much the course has changed to better meet the needs of your program.

Keys to Success with Create-Your-Own Courses

If you find yourself in a program that is creating its own courses, it's wise to get involved as a course author early on. After all, you'll be the one who is spending every day in a class. If it's a class that you created from scratch, you will have fewer edits to make as the year goes on and you'll be happier with the final product.

If you are starting the year with a course that was built by someone within your organization, you will want to follow the same process listed under ''Keys to Success with Purchased Curriculum.'' It's important to know your course inside and out and be able to improve on it each time you teach it.

I should also mention that there are programs out there that expect their teachers to write a course and teach it at the same time. Although it's possible to do that, it is an enormous burden to place on a teacher. If teachers are required to write course content each week in addition to working with students, the level of service to students inevitably suffers. Writing a course is an enormous undertaking. I would anticipate that course writing alone would take twenty to twenty-five hours of every week so the teacher's time to grade assignments, provide feedback, facilitate discussions, and work one-on-one with students would be severely limited. Organizations that attempt this model should limit the teachers' student load significantly for that first year while they are building courses. Writing courses is a creative act and it requires a serious time commitment.

TEACHER AS COURSE AUTHOR AND ORGANIZER VERSUS TEACHER AS FACILITATOR ONLY

In the previous variable, ''Create-Your-Own Versus a Purchased Curriculum,'' I assumed that the teacher had edit and course author privileges within a course.

However, that's not always the case. In some programs, teachers are discouraged or even outright prohibited from making changes in a course. This is an unfortunate practice because it communicates a lack of trust in teachers and also limits a teacher's ability to customize for student needs. However, it's something you may find yourself having to deal with in your teaching situation.

Keys to Success When You Have Course Edit Privileges

When you have edit privileges within a course, it's important that you respect that privilege and follow the mantra, "Do no harm!" Any changes that you make should be because they make a significant improvement in the quality of the course for students. Your changes should also align well with your school's curriculum as well as national and state standards. For more information on creating quality assignments and making positive course modifications, see chapter 8.

When you find yourself with course edit privileges, there's also the issue of being able to keep those changes for following years. In an ideal situation, all teachers who are teaching a particular course will collaborate on course changes. Then all teachers start with the same **master course** (the starting copy of a course for any given semester) at the beginning of each year with the new changes incorporated. That way you can maintain the integrity of the course and also allow for modifications. If all teachers make a variety of modifications and never reconcile those changes to the master course, eventually all the teachers will be teaching completely different versions of the class. Collaboration is key throughout.

Keys to Success When You Are a Facilitator Only

You may find yourself in a teaching situation in which you are required to teach a course exactly as written. An initial question to ask might be whether or not you can add content. Sometimes teachers are allowed to add new content but not delete content. In that case, you can add collaborative elements to the class via a course website, wiki, or other interactive tool. If you are not allowed to add content, you can still enrich a student's experience through being the best possible course facilitator. That means reaching out to students, making relationships, and leading students through the course with excellence. Even if you're not allowed to modify content for students, you can still challenge students to excellence through the feedback you provide on assignments and the way you interact with them in e-mails, phone calls, text messages, and so on.

TEACHER PERFORMANCE (AND PERHAPS PAY) BASED ON COURSE COMPLETION VERSUS BASED ON RUBRIC OR EVALUATION SYSTEMS

Another common variable in online learning, because of teacher accountability programs, is that teachers are sometimes paid according to course completion rather than being paid on the basis of a traditional evaluation system. There are benefits to both options. In a system in which teachers are paid according to course completion, teachers are extremely motivated to make sure their students are successful. They are more likely to contact students regularly and go out of their way to help students catch up once they fall behind. However, many times whether or not a student is successful is due to factors outside the teacher's control. Students may enter with below-grade-level skills or they may have factors in their personal lives that make success impossible. In that case, it can feel unfair for a teacher to be penalized.

In a system in which teachers are hired and paid according to a traditional evaluation system, administrators are able to get a greater feel for the teacher's abilities, regardless of student completion percentages. The system as a whole is also far more likely to look at data points beyond completion percentages. Factors such as student engagement, standardized test scores, and teacher professionalism are all important and should be included in a school's improvement plan, regardless of how teachers get paid. However, under traditional evaluation systems, online learning can be difficult to evaluate. Because there is no classroom to observe, administrators have to improvise to evaluate the online teacher. As a result, sometimes those evaluations are invalid or unreliable indicators of student success.

Keys to Success When Teacher Performance Is Evaluated Based on Course Completion

One of the most important things you can do when your performance (or even your pay) is based on student completion is to remember that doing the things that create quality online learning experiences for students will also make more students successful. When you have a strong relationship with students because you have contacted them, provided in-depth feedback, talked with them regularly, and shown them that you care, they are more likely to succeed in your course. When you build a classroom community for students using facilitated discussions, group projects, and shared norms, students are more likely to care about your class. As a result, they are more likely to succeed. Although it can be tempting in an environment in which you are judged solely on course completion statistics to focus only on numbers and finding ways to improve those numbers, the big picture is still important. If you are a high-quality teacher, your methods will prove themselves over time. Offer your students the best in high-quality online learning and don't let failures (either yours or your students) cloud your focus.

Keys to Success in Traditional Evaluation Systems

When you find yourself being evaluated as an online teacher by a traditional teacher's model, it can be frustrating simply because online teaching so often breaks the mold. In my first evaluation as an online teacher, the administrator was limited to judging me based solely on the quality of my once-a-week synchronous sessions for students (webinars). There was no mechanism to evaluate anything else I was doing, such as communicating with students, providing assessment feedback, building course content, or facilitating discussions, so the administration had to focus on the only thing I did that looked like a traditional teacher: synchronous webinars. Even then, items on the rubric such as ''discipline by proximity'' and ''eye contact'' were not applicable. We made the best we could of the situation. Since then, my program has started to implement some other ways of evaluating online teachers' work. Other programs across the country are beginning that pioneering work also.

As a teacher doing a nontraditional job in a traditional system, your greatest responsibility should be to make the work you do in an online classroom as visible as possible. Invite administrators to tour your online classroom and see what you do. Copy them on e-mails that you send to students (or that they send to you) so that they can see the positive impact you're making. More than anything be an advocate for online teachers. Talk about what you do with people and let them see your passion. That will go a long way toward advancing our field and toward creating positive evaluations.

WHAT KIND OF ONLINE OR BLENDED TEACHING MODEL IS RIGHT FOR YOU?

You can see why the field of online teaching is so complex. These variables and many others make up the enormous variety that you might find in any given online teaching position. The key is, first of all, to consider all the variables before you take an online teaching job. You need to fully understand the complexities of the teaching situation and decide whether or not they can match up with your strengths and teaching philosophy. Second, once you find yourself in a teaching position, you must make the best of your situation. You often won't have any control over a given program's philosophy or structure. What you do have control over is how you work within that structure to create excellent learning opportunities

Table 1.2   Variables in a Digital Classroom

Variable	Option One	Option Two
How students move through course content	Self-paced online program	Cohort-based online program
How students receive the majority of their courses	Full-time online students	Part-time online students
How course content is delivered	Blended delivery of instruction	Fully online delivery of instruction
How course content is created	Course content created by local teachers	Course content purchased from a third-party vendor
How teacher interacts with course content	Teacher has full course edit privileges	Teacher does not have course edit privileges
How teacher is evaluated	Teacher evaluated and paid based on course completion	Teacher evaluated in a traditional evaluation system

for students. Just as in a face-to-face-classroom, a quality teacher makes all the difference.

Table 1.2 provides a matrix illustrating the variables in this chapter. Take a moment and circle the descriptors that fit your current teaching situation or prospective teaching situation. If you have not yet found an online teaching job, you may want to fill it out for what your ideal situation might be. It can be a great way to evaluate a given teaching job and consider your personal philosophies on online learning. Note that although the variables are represented as a dichotomy you may find situations in which the reality is somewhere between the two options.

FOCUS ON BLENDED LEARNING

When considering a blended teaching situation, most of the variables in this chapter will still apply. However, you'll also have a couple of additional variables you'll need to consider.

The first variable is the issue of how much class time is in a classroom and how much is online. You'll need to have a full understanding of how much class time is required for your students. Are students coming in once a week to a classroom?

What if they're coming in to a classroom every day except on Fridays, when they work online? Those distinctions will make a big difference in your teaching situation and in the way you approach the class.

The second variable you'll want to add in a blended teaching situation is whether teachers are working fully from a classroom or if their work time can be spent at least partially at home. In a blended environment, students are spending some time in the classroom and some time working from home or in a computer lab; teachers may also be offered that flexibility. That distinction will make a huge difference in your working environment. It's important to understand the expectations from the beginning.

CHAPTER TWO

COURSE PHILOSOPHY

ESSENTIAL QUESTIONS:

- What makes a good online learning experience for students and teachers?
- What elements should I look for when evaluating the effectiveness of an online course?
- How can I tell if students are engaged with my course content?

When talking to people about online learning, everyone will have a horror story to tell you. They'll talk about an online course that felt like they had to "jump through hoops." They'll talk about an online course in which the professor or teacher was completely disconnected from the course experience. They'll talk about an online course in which they did nothing but read a textbook and post to a **discussion board** (a space in an LMS where students can have a written discussion about a particular topic). There are many iterations of online learning and quality varies significantly. What we need as online educators is a lens to use when evaluating the online learning experience. We need a course philosophy that helps us think about what makes a good course as well as how we can create that course for our students.

When I first began writing online courses, my primary concern was content. I wanted to make sure that the content for a class was visually appealing and mentally stimulating. What I realized in those first experiences is that good content is not enough to make an engaging course. There needs to be a lot more going on in a course to make it a good experience for students. After taking a course on how to be an online facilitator, I started thinking about my course in terms of three

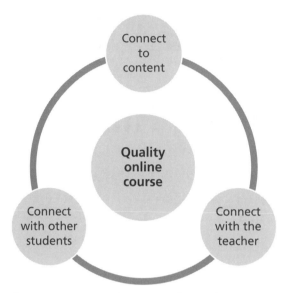

Figure 2.1 Connections in Quality Online Courses

basic connections, which is a simplified version of a model of online education first proposed by Terry Anderson (2008) in *The Theory and Practice of Online Learning*. First, I want students connected to content. Second, I want students connected with each other. Finally, I want students connected with me. When all of those elements are working together, students have a far stronger learning experience. Figure 2.1 provides an overview for that course philosophy.

CONNECT TO CONTENT

The first element to consider in the course philosophy is the connection to content. We want students to have a high-quality encounter with the content of the course. When they leave the course, they should be able to explain in-depth how they have grown as learners. That means avoiding some of the pitfalls explained earlier: courses that don't require critical thinking, courses that have no variety, and courses that don't include student choice. Instead, the course content should have these critical elements:

- Content that values collaboration, communication, and creativity
- Content that is "un-Googleable"
- Content that includes student choice in every unit

Content That Values Collaboration, Communication, and Creativity

As students we didn't appreciate teachers who just had us read and take multiple choice exams. Those classes were boring. Too often in online education we have used a similar course philosophy, especially with self-paced and credit-recovery courses. For some reason online course designers seem to have thought that just putting content like that online would make it more engaging. It's not. We still have to think in terms of good pedagogy and we still have to think about how we will make the course engaging for students.

The English 10 course I started with included a lot of grammar quizzes. Basically, students were reading content about grammar rules and then applying those rules within a multiple choice quiz. It was an expedient way to review grammar but it wasn't particularly engaging. I needed a new way to help students engage with content. Instead of using multiple choice quizzes in all those grammar lessons, I introduced the students to Grammar Girl (http://grammar.quickanddirtytips.com). Grammar Girl produces a regular podcast on grammar topics. However, she does it in an engaging way. Her tone is light and funny. She's informal about the rules and shares some really hilarious examples of grammar errors. After listening to several of her podcasts, my students are tasked with creating their own Grammar Girl–style podcasts. They write a script about the grammar topic we're studying and then use the podcast tool within our LMS to produce their own podcast on a **voiceboard** (a discussion board that allows them to use voice tools). Once that's complete, they listen to each other's podcasts and critique them. Instead of a sit-and-get model of online education, they're actively involved in producing content and, along the way, they learn grammar rules in a really memorable way. Their learning is more engaging, more memorable, and even stretches beyond the standards for the course. They've learned more than grammar skills. They've learned how to communicate and be creative with content.

Content That Is Un-Googleable

Un-Googleable content is content that can't easily be found using a search engine. If I were to ask my students to write a paper on the significance of color in *The Great Gatsby*, they could easily find all sorts of information on that within Google or any search engine. In fact, the search ''significance of color in *The Great Gatsby*'' yields 89,600 hits via Google. In order to complete that paper, students would not have to think critically about the novel. They'd just need to read a few websites and compile the information. If my goal in this assignment is to have students analyze the text, what about having them create a fictional dialogue between Gatsby and Elisa, a main character in ''The Chrysanthemums'' (another short story we read within that unit)? Students would have to consider what these two characters have in common and what they might discuss if they met face-to-face. They're immediately going to have to consider theme and characterization before they can even begin to prewrite this assignment. They can't find it on Google and therefore will have to think critically about both texts. It's a far more valuable learning experience and one that's more lasting.

Creating un-Googleable assignments also means updating course content on a regular basis. Students are smart. If a course is taught to several hundred students in the same way every semester, it will, in a very short time, become Googleable. Students will post the assignments to Yahoo! Answers or a similar resource and other students will find it. It's up to the teacher or content developer to continually update those assignments so that they stay fresh and off the Internet radar.

Content That Includes Student Choice in Every Unit

Although content standards must stay the same for every student, there is a lot of variety that can be built in for how students demonstrate knowledge of those standards. Students in a science class can demonstrate their understanding of mitosis by creating a video, writing and performing a song, or creating an animation. The content standards remain the same but students are demonstrating their knowledge of them in a way that's interesting to them. When students have choices about how to demonstrate their learning, they're more likely to be engaged with the content and achieve at a high level.

My students sometimes get to choose their own novel for a unit. I'll provide a list of grade-level-appropriate texts that all have something in common (theme, genre, and so on). Then they'll choose the novel that's most interesting to them. Over the course of a unit, I'm still teaching about the literary terms I'm required to cover (such as theme, characterization, and so on) but they have a choice in the text they're using to demonstrate that knowledge.

Students tend to complain less about something they chose themselves. I recently had a student who chose *Great Expectations* for her novel in a unit focused on characterization. This is a difficult text for high school students because they have such a hard time connecting to the characters. When I asked the student what she thought of the novel, she said, ''Well, it's really hard but I chose it because it's a classic and I wanted to challenge myself. I'm sticking with my choice and I'm proud that I've been able to read it.'' The power of choice makes a huge difference for learning.

CONNECT WITH OTHER STUDENTS

The second element to consider in the course philosophy is the connection to other students. The fact of the matter is that we are social beings. When we feel isolated, we're less likely to be committed to an activity. If it's just me and a computer sitting in a room, it doesn't matter if I put off working in that class until next week, next month, or next year. However, if I feel like I'm a part of something larger than myself, I'm more likely to do my part. If I feel like I'm part of a classroom community, I'm more likely to connect to my course content and participate on a regular basis. I'm more likely to have success.

Helping students to connect with each other doesn't happen by accident. The first step during **zero week** (the first week of an online course—covered in more depth in chapter 4 on building relationships) is that students introduce themselves in the discussion board. They share pictures and tidbits about themselves. They respond to other posts. They find other students who love Van Halen or Muppets movies. They make connections with other students. It's the same sort of thing that might happen during a passing period of a traditional school. Students are getting connected so they feel like a community.

Once the sense of classroom culture has been developed during that first week, students are engaged with each other on a weekly or biweekly basis through facilitated threaded discussions in our LMS. Every subject (even math!) has topics that lend themselves to discussion. Open-ended discussion questions can get students talking to each other and help deepen their learning. Here are just a few examples of successful discussion prompts:

- *Math*: The concept of zero is attributed to mathematicians in India around the ninth century. Before that the Greeks decided against creating a zero in math because they weren't sure how *nothing* could actually equate to *something*. Why do you think it took so long for someone to begin using zero in math? How would math be different if we didn't have the concept of zero?

- *English*: Pretend you are an advice columnist. You have just received this letter from Hamlet:

  Dear Abby,

  My name is Hamlet. I've just been visited by a ghost who claims to be my father. He says that my uncle killed him so that he could steal the throne of Denmark and marry my mother. I'm not sure if I should trust the ghost or not. To make matters worse, I tried talking to my mother about the situation and wound up killing my ex-girlfriend's father. What should I do?

Sincerely,

Hamlet

On the discussion board, write a 100- to 150-word response in which you tell Hamlet what he should do next.

- *History:* The framers of the Constitution struggled significantly with how to provide equal representation to the states. They eventually came up with the two houses of Congress, one focused on representation by population and one focused on representation by state. How would our system of government be different if we had only the Senate and no House of Representatives?

These discussions are facilitated by the teacher and provide a place for students to discuss the content on a deeper level with their peers. They are a stand-in for the intangibles that happen during a face-to-face class. Students are challenging each other's thinking and taking that content knowledge to a deeper place than if they were just learning alone. (Discussion board strategies and facilitation are covered in more depth in chapter 6.)

In addition to facilitated discussions, students also work together on group projects. Digital tools provide some opportunities for collaboration that are simply not available in a face-to-face classroom. I recently had my students create a wiki demonstrating their knowledge of grammar concepts. A **wiki** is just a web page that is very easy for multiple people to edit. I created the shell of the wiki with blank pages for information on commas, information on run-ons, videos about grammar concepts, grammar games, and so on. Then my students, in my tenth- and twelfth-grade classes, were responsible for working together to create a complete grammar wiki that could be used as a resource throughout the course when any student was struggling with a particular grammar concept. Not only were they learning grammar content while creating this wiki, they were also challenging each other and creating something that was bigger and deeper than anything they could have created on their own. A similar project could be created for almost any content area and subtopic. Group projects are covered in more depth in chapter 9 and they are an amazing way to help students learn together in the online space.

Finally, students are connecting with each other in live virtual sessions. These are sessions that are held once a week using a webinar-style tool. (A **webinar** is a synchronous session within a course in which students can get together in real time with the teacher and discuss course content.) We all touch base during that time. Kids can share how things are going in their lives as well as in my class. I make it a safe space where we laugh and tease as well as learn content. We have discussions as well as minilessons during that time.

When students are connected to each other, the learning is deeper than it could be when they're on their own. They're challenging each other's thinking and therefore are learning more than they ever could in isolation.

CONNECT WITH THE TEACHER

The final element to consider in a quality course philosophy is the connection with a teacher. I'm often asked by reporters if I think my job as an online educator will disappear in the next twenty years. The implication is that someday I might be replaced completely by a computer. My emphatic response has always been, "Absolutely not." I wholeheartedly believe that teachers are the most important element in any online classroom. They are the ones behind the scenes who are challenging students to excellence. A computer, no matter how sophisticated, cannot do that work because it is very personal work and different for every student's needs. I know my student's stories. I know their skills. I know how to customize their learning experience. I am their teacher and that's an absolutely vital role if online learning is to be successful.

When I first began teaching online, I had the opportunity to take over two online classes mid-semester. In one, the teacher left to take another position. She had been a responsible online teacher: posting announcements, keeping up with due dates, communicating with students, providing feedback on assignments, and so on. The transition to a new teacher was easy. The students were engaged with the course and they just had someone else leading the way.

In the other, the teacher had gotten overwhelmed by the workload. She stopped communicating with students or doing any of the other best practices of online instructors. Whether she was a victim of circumstance or a lack of training, I don't know, but she was removed from her course. The transition was very difficult. The students were all over the place. They had no connection to the course or with each other. Many had simply given up.

The contrast between these two situations highlights the need for a connected, competent teacher in the online classroom. Any student, but especially a young student, needs the guiding hand of a responsible adult who knows the material and pushes him or her to succeed. Without that connection, students will flounder.

The question then becomes, "How do online teachers create a connection with a student they've never met face-to-face?" It all starts at the beginning of a course. The first step in any course should be a student survey. Give students the opportunity to introduce themselves to you, the teacher. Ask them if there's anything going on in their lives that might affect how they will perform in class. Ask them how they've done with past classes in the subject area. Ask them to set goals for their learning in that semester. There are some example questions in chapter 4. The amazing thing is that kids will open up online in ways they never will face-to-face. There's not the pressure of thirty other students sitting in the classroom listening. There's just a student and a caring adult. You learn their story and from that learn what you need to do to engage them in your class.

From that initial survey, the relationship continues to develop through feedback on assignments. When assignments are carefully crafted to engage students in critical thinking, it becomes obvious early on what a student's skills are like. The teacher's job is then to build on those skills. Feedback on assignments should focus on specific skills that students need to work on. From that customized, personal feedback, students can begin to improve their understanding of the course content. Only a teacher who knows the student's story as well as his or her skills can give the student the kind of feedback needed to grow. A letter grade and canned comments simply can't do the same kind of work. (For more information on providing feedback see chapter 11.)

In addition to providing feedback on assignments, the student's connection with the teacher also grows through regular communication. Everyone has a communication preference. Some students prefer e-mail, some prefer text messaging, some prefer phone calls. It's up to the teacher to find out that preferred method and then touch base with students regularly. Kids need a caring adult in order to grow academically. The online teacher's job is to constantly say (literally and figuratively), ''I see you. I know you're there. I care about you. I can help.'' That constant communication helps students to know that they matter and it also helps them to remember to work regularly in the course.

Finally, the online teacher has to connect with students using multiple roles. Sometimes the teacher will be a life coach, helping students to set goals for the semester and create plans to carry them out. Sometimes the teacher will be a cheerleader, helping students see what's possible and letting them know that they really can do it. Sometimes the teacher will be a counselor, letting students know that she cares about them and getting them the help and resources they need for their particular situation. Other times the teacher acts solely as tutor, helping break down content in a way that makes sense for a student's learning style. The experienced teacher is comfortable in all these roles and moves fluidly between them depending on the student's needs.

CONNECTING ON ALL THREE FRONTS

When students are connected to the course content, connected with each other, and connected with the teacher, they truly care about the class. They're motivated to be successful. If any one of these elements is missing, it's still possible to have a valuable learning experience; however, the course experience is not as good as it could have been. It's like driving with a flat tire. You might still reach your destination but it won't be easy!

As online educators, it is our responsibility to make sure that every learning experience challenges students to achieve excellence. Creating these three connections to content, with other students, and with the teacher can help make that happen and improve learning for students.

FOCUS ON BLENDED LEARNING

The basic course philosophy presented in this chapter can also be easily applied in a blended learning environment. With the benefit of some face-to-face time, students can build even stronger connections with one another and with the teacher during the time they are in the physical classroom. However, it's important to ensure that some of those connections are also happening in the online space. The types of connections that build in a digital space are often of a different quality and depth than what we might develop in a forty-five-minute class period. It can be tempting to limit student-to-student connections and student-to-teacher connections to the physical space only, without also deepening those connections in the online environment. If you do that, the online portion of your course could become simply an online textbook for accessing content rather than a robust learning environment. It's essential to make sure that the online and face-to-face components of your course contain all three elements of a strong course: student-to-content connections, student-with-student connections, and student-with-teacher connections.

CHAPTER THREE

PREPARING TO TEACH AN ONLINE COURSE

ESSENTIAL QUESTIONS:

- How should an online course be organized to maximize success?

- How does a syllabus for an online course differ from a traditional course?

- How can I manage student contact information in an efficient manner?

- How does the first week of a course differ from the rest?

- How can I set up my students for success?

Think back to the summer before your first face-to-face teaching assignment. There were a lot of decisions to consider: What units should I start with first? How will I get to know my students quickly? How should I arrange the furniture in my classroom? What kind of grading policies should I have in place? How will I stay organized? In many ways, the first time teaching online entails very similar decisions. Instead of thinking about which unit to start first, an online teacher might spend time cleaning up the first unit and hiding all the other units that students won't need right away. Instead of thinking about how to get to know students quickly, the online teacher will build discussion forums and collect student information that will facilitate communication. Instead of thinking about how to arrange the furniture, the online teacher will think about how to arrange the navigation of the course. What remains the same is that a quality teacher is always planning for success. The more time and effort you put into your course before you begin teaching it, the more successful the course will be.

COURSE ORGANIZATION

Some of the most critical decisions you will make in your online course are how to organize your course content for success. There's an art to organizing a course so that it is intuitive for students. On the one hand, you want everything to be easily accessible from the main page. On the other hand, you don't want to overwhelm students with too many buttons so they're not sure where to begin. *Note*: The term *button* is used throughout this chapter as a tool that students click on to navigate through a course. However, in your LMS, the term *folder* may make more sense.

Your very first task should be to take a quick walkthrough of your LMS as it's currently configured. Take a look at the navigation of the main pages. Pretend you are a student who knows nothing about online learning. Would you be able to find the assignments? Would you be able to find your teacher's contact information? Is the information there overwhelming or do you feel you could navigate through it? Once you've looked at the course through a critical lens, start creating a flowchart for how you want your course to operate (see the sample in figure 3.1). Items on the left are first-level navigation items, accessible from the main page. Items on the right are second-level navigation items, accessible after clicking on a first-level navigation button.

As a part of your flowchart, you may find that you want to elevate items from second-level navigation (accessible from under another button) to a first-level button. For example, the course calendar is a very important part of a class so it may make more sense for it to be readily available on the main page rather than having to go to the course info button and then to the calendar to find it, as shown in the sample flow chart. Also, if you are teaching a course that is very discussion heavy, you may want to make a button on the main page for just discussion boards because students will access those on a regular basis. Remember that first-level items should be the absolute most important items that you know students will need on a regular basis.

As a general rule, you should avoid having more than about ten to twelve buttons on your main page. Fewer are generally better because it makes the course easier to navigate. All other content should be found under another button. Figure 3.2 is a screenshot of one of my courses and its navigation buttons.

You can see that I have elevated the calendar, discussion board, and grades tools to first-level navigation so that they're easy to find. I also like having the

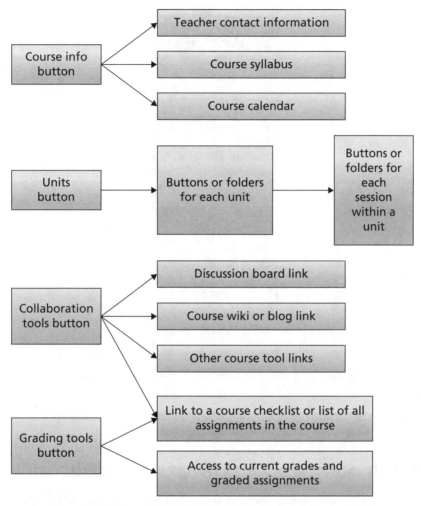

Figure 3.1   Sample Flowchart of How to Organize an LMS

teacher info button prominently displayed so that students don't have to hunt to find my contact information. Although there are currently two units displayed in the navigation bar, I sometimes leave more available if I have several students who are working in older units or if students need to access old assignments in order to complete their current work. I also have added subheadings to the navigation pane so that the organization of the buttons is clearer.

At first it may seem as if you are spending an inordinate amount of time simply organizing content for your class. However, it is time well spent. Once a course has begun, you should avoid moving content buttons if at all possible. Students

Figure 3.2   Current Course Navigation Buttons Example

come to rely on finding the discussion board button in a particular spot and if you move it, they'll become confused and frustrated.

FLESHING OUT THE COURSE INFORMATION BUTTON

Once you have a basic course structure created, it's time to start adding content to the course information button (or its equivalent). Basically, the course information area is where students can come to find information on grading policies, due dates, teacher contact information, and so on. It's vital that this information be current as well as complete.

Teacher Information

The first and most vital piece of information you will add to your course is the teacher information. At a minimum, your teacher information area should include your name, a picture, an e-mail address, a phone number, information on office hours, and a brief introduction. You want your profile to be welcoming for students. It can be intimidating for them to contact a complete stranger so it's important that you make it as easy as possible.

As far as contact information goes, you want the information in your teacher profile to be something you check regularly. Your e-mail address should be a professional address provided by your employer if at all possible. For your phone number, you should let students know what times it is OK to contact you. Otherwise you *will* get calls at 11:30 P.M.! You'll also need to think about what phone number would be best to share with students. A personal cell phone number can be OK if you're always careful about how you answer the phone and where. However, if you'd like more separation between your work life and personal life, it can be a good idea to get a business line for managing calls from students. I personally use Google Voice as my work phone number. It gives me an alternate phone number for students to use but I can forward it to my cell phone or any other number when I'm working. There's more information about Google Voice in chapter 12.

The picture you use should be professional but also friendly. I took one early in my first year of online teaching that I post everywhere for students to see. I want them to know who's behind the computer working with them!

The welcome message that you include in your teacher profile should be brief but should also give students an idea of who you are. It can be a good idea to include information about your family, interests, why you're a teacher, and so on. The whole purpose is to let students know that you're a real person. Exhibit 3.1 shows the introduction note I'm currently using on my teacher profile.

Exhibit 3.1. Sample Welcome Message

Welcome to our course! I'm so glad you've joined us.

My name is Kristin Kipp and I'll be the facilitator of this course.

I've been a teacher for about ten years now, focusing on English and language arts with eighth- through twelfth-graders. I absolutely love getting to work with young people. It's such a thrill to see someone learn something new. Online learning is especially exciting because the Internet opens up our world to so many extraordinary possibilities.

Becoming an English teacher was a natural extension of my favorite hobby: reading. I'm an avid reader, with interests ranging from theories of education to backpacking. Lately I've also been using the Internet to expand my reading even further. Websites such as Ning and GoodReads allow me to interact with other readers and discuss the new ideas I'm learning about. Writing about reading definitely forces you to take your analysis to a much deeper level. As a result, my critical reading and writing abilities have grown exponentially. It's an experience I hope you'll have too as we start our work together on this course.

I'm looking forward to our time together. You can expect to be challenged as you wrestle with some new ideas and learn some new skills. It's hard work but also very rewarding. Let me know how I can support you! If you have questions, please feel free to e-mail me. Thanks!

Syllabus

Once you have your teacher information area filled out, it's time to start thinking about the syllabus for your course. In general, syllabi for online courses are longer than a traditional syllabus. Most traditional teachers spend a class period going over the syllabus along with grading policies and expectations. In an online classroom, the syllabus itself needs to convey all the clarifying information that you might usually have explained verbally. Everything needs to go in writing so that your expectations are clear. However, your syllabus will probably contain similar information to a face-to-face syllabus. Following is a list of topics to consider covering in your syllabus, with ones that are unique to online learning marked with an asterisk:

- Overview of the course

- Approximate due dates for various units and major projects

- Contact information for the teacher* (more detailed in online learning)

- Information on office hours and synchronous sessions*

- Materials needed

- Course expectations

- Grading policies

- Late-work policies

- Attendance policies (if applicable)* (may vary depending on your online format)

- Troubleshooting chart for coping with technical problems*

- Information about academic integrity and plagiarism* (focused on online learning concerns)

- Information on netiquette*

- Discussion board expectations*

In appendix B you will find a syllabus that I'm currently using with my students. It can give you an idea of where to begin and what kind of depth is needed in a syllabus for an online course.

Many of the decisions about your grading policies will be personal decisions dependent on your teaching philosophy and also your program's teaching model. For example, I enforce a late-work policy within my courses. Students can earn 75 percent credit for late assignments within the current unit. Once we are past a unit, that unit is closed to late work. Because we run a cohort system, students generally pace through the course together with weekly deadlines. I believe that students need to be accountable for due dates because the real world requires that you adhere to a strict work schedule with clear deadlines. I want students to experience that kind of accountability in my classroom so that it won't be a shock when they enter the work world full-time. However, other teachers in my program do not enforce late-work policies. They assign due dates but will take work from any point in the course at any time without penalty. I respect their decision to do that because I know they are focused on student success. As you write your syllabus, you'll want to consider your own philosophies on deadlines, grading, late work, and attendance and make sure that your expectations in your syllabus clearly line up with your own values and the requirements of your school.

Also keep in mind as you create your syllabus that the value of online learning is its flexibility. Although I lay out some pretty strict guidelines in my course syllabus, I am flexible with those policies depending on a particular student's needs. I recently worked with a student who was put into foster care after her first month in my class. She got very behind in class because she was being shuffled from home to home, sometimes without Internet access, and was constantly worried about moving back in with her family. At that point, my grading policies had to go out the window. This was a student who needed flexibility and because of the online course environment I was able to provide that for her. She finished the semester with a C but only because I was willing to let her work in past units and I provided a critical path for her to show progress in the course. (There's more information on using critical paths with students in chapter 10.) In some ways your course syllabus needs to adhere to the old teaching maxim, ''Don't smile until Christmas.'' Provide high expectations and rigid policies for your students in your syllabus but then be willing to bend those policies when necessary (just as you would do in the face-to-face classroom).

Students should be required to read the course syllabus during the first week of class. Some teachers also have them take a quiz about the syllabus. Multiple choice questions on topics such as, ''How much credit is given for late work?'' can ensure that students are reading the syllabus and that they understand it. I also usually have the students answer a yes or no question saying, ''I have read the course syllabus and I understand the course policies.'' That way, if there are problems with a policy later, you have it on record that the student read the syllabus and understood it.

Calendar

The final element you'll want to flesh out in your course information area is your course calendar. The way you build your calendar will vary depending on the model of online learning that your school uses. However, at a minimum you should have a course calendar that indicates general due dates for each session and unit as well as times for synchronous sessions and office hours. Your students should be able to plan out at least the next month of their course work and deadlines using your calendar, whether you are using hard deadlines or more soft suggested deadlines. Other information such as testing, parent-teacher conferences, and so on should also be included. Students should have a clear understanding about what's coming up.

Most LMSs will have some sort of calendar function built in. If the function is used consistently by all staff members, the calendar can usually populate all upcoming due dates from all courses onto one calendar. Because time management is often one of the biggest struggles for online students, having a functional calendar with all deadlines available can be a huge help. Google Calendar is a great option for this. Each teacher creates a public Google Calendar for his or her course and then shares that link with students. Then students can add each course calendar to their own Google Calendar, providing a one-stop destination for all course due dates as well as personal events. Students appreciate having access to everything in one place. The biggest key is to make sure that all teachers are using the same calendar tool in the same way so that students know how to find the information they need in all their classes at any time.

BE VOCAL, AN ACRONYM FOR TEACHER SUCCESS

John Savery, in a 2005 article for the *Journal of Interactive Online Learning*, created an acronym for how to be successful as an online teacher. He says that online teachers should be VOCAL: visible, organized, compassionate, analytical, and leaders-by-example. As you prepare to teach your online course, it's worthwhile to take a moment and think through how you will include each of these elements:

- *Visible:* To be visible as an online teacher means that you are purposefully present in a course. You are posting to the discussion boards, adding announcements, and so forth so that students know you're an active participant (and that you're there to help). If you are logging in every day and reading all the posts or assignments but you're not responding to them, students don't know that you're present in the course. You have to purposefully make your work visible.

- *Organized:* To be organized as an online teacher means that you have a well-developed course that is easy to navigate. Learners understand the expectations and know how to find the information they need.

- *Compassionate:* To be compassionate as an online teacher means that you are willing to be flexible to meet students' needs. Students will come to your course with a variety of learning needs and you'll sometimes need to bend the rules a bit to help meet them.

- *Analytical:* To be analytical as an online teacher means that you are using the plethora of information from your LMS to monitor student work and draw conclusions about their needs. There's a ton of data available in an online classroom but the data are only useful if the online teacher is watching and modifying instruction accordingly.

- *Leader-by-example:* The online teacher leads by example in all aspects of a course. By answering e-mails quickly and in a friendly, professional tone, you're modeling to students the kinds of communication you expect. When you post to a discussion board in a way that is thoughtful and builds the discussion, you're showing students how to participate in a discussion and the kinds of posts you expect.

As you prepare yourself for teaching a given course, it's important to think through all the elements of the ''be VOCAL'' acronym and consider how you might emphasize them in your instruction.

A WORD TO THE WISE

The tasks listed in this chapter, such as creating a solid course organization, building a great syllabus, using a course calendar, will set up your course for success. Your students will be far more likely to have a positive initial impression and therefore are far more likely to succeed. However, you should also realize that there will be things you will forget. Every year I find something that I want to change for the next time I teach a course. An assignment doesn't work, I find

I don't like the location of a button, and so on. Always remember that's part of the process of teaching, even online teaching. One of the tough things about online courses is that your missteps are very visible but they're also correctable. Give yourself permission to make mistakes and grow, just as you would your students. You can always regroup for next semester and try something new!

FOCUS ON BLENDED LEARNING

When preparing to teach a blended course, there are some additional considerations. One is to set some parameters for how much of a course is online. If students are spending 50 percent of their class time in a classroom and 50 percent online, then you'll want to make sure your course work is built accordingly. Each online session should replace approximately 50 percent of the instruction of that unit. The grading should match that percentage also, whenever possible. Thus, 50 percent of the grading should be based on online sessions and 50 percent on face-to-face work.

Teacher Brooke Fabian of East Boston High School has 15 percent of her student's grade based on online elements, which are accessed only as homework and not as part of the regular course content. She says she had to create the exact percentage so that students knew that the online elements were an important part of her course and thus would pay attention to doing well there.

You'll also want to make some plans for how you'll introduce the online elements of your course to your students. If possible, make some time to explore the tools together during a face-to-face session. If you do a lot of troubleshooting and explaining up front, the online portion of your class will run more smoothly throughout.

CHAPTER FOUR

BUILDING RELATIONSHIPS WITH STUDENTS

ESSENTIAL QUESTIONS:

- How does an online teacher get to know his or her students?
- How can I manage student data in an effective way?
- What is a zero week?
- How do I communicate who I am as a teacher in my online course?
- What role do face-to-face events play in an online course?

As I reflect on my years teaching online, there are relationships that I have built with students that have meant the world to me. I think of Marie. Marie joined our school as a junior in high school. Her freshman year of high school, she missed more than sixty days of school due to health problems. Her sophomore year, her dad passed away. Suddenly Marie didn't feel she belonged in high school anymore. No one understood what she was going through and the high school drama just didn't work for her. Marie was on the verge of dropping out and, in fact, took a semester off school. Thankfully, Marie's mother refused to give up on her. She continued to search for options to help Marie graduate. She found our online program and helped Marie get enrolled. During that first semester, I built a strong relationship with Marie. I found out about her story and cheered on every little success. When she told me that my course was too easy for her, I modified her course content and worked with her on an independent study. Because of our relationship and the ones she had with all of her other teachers, Marie was able to reconnect with school. This bright, promising eighteen-year-old was almost failed by our school system but, because of an online school and the relationships she built there, she was able to graduate high school and, not just graduate, but graduate as the valedictorian of her class.

In the last chapter, we focused primarily on the computer and course side of getting ready to teach a course. However, online teaching, just like face-to-face teaching, is really about working with people. It's about working with students like Marie who have complex lives and complex stories. Students you have never met face-to-face still have very real lives and, as an online teacher, it's your job to get to know them. In this chapter, we'll explore how to create those relationships with students and use the teacher-student relationship to challenge students to success.

STARTING AT THE BEGINNING

Building relationships with students starts from the very first day (or before). Students need to hear from you early and often. You need to find ways to connect with kids and let them know that you care about them from the very beginning. Strategies such as an initial course survey, welcome phone calls, and zero week can help you get to know your students and help them get to know you. When students have a strong relationship with their teacher from the beginning they are far more likely to succeed throughout the course.

Initial Course Survey

One of the first assignments that your students should participate in is an initial course survey. The survey is a chance for students to share about themselves with their teacher. Tools such as Survey Monkey can be a great way to gather that data, but your LMS probably also has a tool for gathering survey data from students. Google Forms is another excellent option with the added bonus that responses are automatically added to an easy-to-navigate spreadsheet. Questions about interests, family background, past school performance, and so on can give you a really good picture of your students from the very beginning. It's amazing how much a student will share with you if you ask in a caring, confidential format.

The course survey should include about eight to ten questions. You'll want to set clear expectations about how long the responses should be. I generally ask for about a paragraph on each question. Then, in addition to getting to know my students, I'm also learning something about their literacy skills. Here are some questions you can consider including in your survey:

- What do you do when you're not working on school? Or what kinds of things are you interested in outside of school?

- Who do you live with and how would you describe your family?

- If someone had to describe you in five words, what five words might they use? Why do those words fit you well?

- If you were stranded on a deserted island and could take only five things with you, what five things would you take and why?

- What's your preferred method of communication (e-mail, text message, phone call, IM, and so on) and why do you prefer that mode over other ways of communicating?

- In general, how have you done in past English (math, social studies, foreign language, and so on) courses?

- What goals do you have for yourself this semester?

- How are you with computers? What are your strengths and weaknesses?

- Have you taken online courses before? What questions or anxieties do you have about working in this online course this semester?

- Is there anything else going on in your life that might affect your schoolwork?

- What kind of support do you need from me (your teacher) in order to be successful in this course?

- What questions do you have before we begin the semester?

It's amazing how much students will share with you when you simply take the time to ask. From the course survey, you can also begin to form a mental picture of your students. You'll know which students are high achievers who will need to be challenged. You'll know which students have struggled with motivation in the past and will need to hear from you regularly. You'll also know which students are likely to fall through the cracks and you can go out of your way to reach out to them. That initial survey is a powerful instructional tool.

Contact Information Database

As a part of the initial course survey, you'll also want to ask students to provide detailed contact information. The student information system is often incorrect or contains only contact information for parents. As an online teacher, you need more detailed contact information and contacts that are specifically for the student, which may or may not be different from the parent. I generally ask for a phone number, a texting number (if it's different from the regular phone number), and a current e-mail address. It's also wise to ask students which is their preferred method of communication. Some students will feel isolated if they don't talk to you on the phone on a regular basis whereas others are happier if you just e-mail or text message them. Some students even prefer instant messaging to any other tool. It's important to know the student's preference and try to accommodate that when possible. I also ask that students commit to checking their e-mail at least once a day while our course is in session. I need to know that I can contact students at any time and can expect a twenty-four-hour response time via e-mail. In return, I promise the same response time for their e-mails to me.

Once initial surveys are in, I download the information and create a special database with student contact information. That database then gets turned into an e-mail distribution list within my e-mail program as well as a text messaging contact list in Google Voice. Those automated systems speed up my communications significantly and ensure that students don't feel isolated. There's more information on setting up communications in chapter 12.

Asking for contact information in the initial course survey also plays a huge role in success with at-risk students. If a student happens to log in just on the first day, fills out the initial survey, and then disappears from your course, you have given yourself some amazing tools for helping to reengage them in the work. You can use that contact information to get them reconnected with what's happening in class. Regular texts, e-mails, and phone calls can go a long way in letting a student know that you care. Although I often refer to myself as a ''professional cyber-stalker,'' for some students that's what they need in order to be successful. I'm happy to use whatever tools I have at my disposal to help students find success.

Welcome Week Synchronous Session

You'll also want to set up a welcome week synchronous session in your class's webinar tool or, at a minimum, a **screencast** of you introducing the class. (A screencast is a video of your screen with a voiceover. Jing is a common tool for this purpose.) This webinar or video is just a time for students to come together as a group and hear your voice. During that session you can share a bit about yourself, provide a course tour, hit the highlights of the course syllabus, and, if you're hosting a webinar, answer any questions that students may have. That synchronous session should be recorded and then stored in a prominent place in the course. Any time students are having trouble with navigation or have come into the class late, they can watch that session as an orientation for class. It's a fantastic way for visual learners to get the hang of online learning and find out about the idiosyncrasies of your class. It also creates a resource that students can refer to later when they need help.

Welcome Calls

Another strategy that can be extremely helpful in getting to know your students is to set up welcome calls with all your students. A five-minute phone call can go a long way in building a relationship and letting your students know that you care about them. Remember that some students will not contact you when they have questions, especially at first. If you contact them first, they're more likely to ask their questions and have success in the course.

If you don't have enough time to call every student, you can also consider just calling those who caught your attention on the course surveys. These are the red-flag students who may have struggled with school in the past or have extenuating circumstances at home. Making an early, personal contact with those students can make a huge difference in their success. They need a caring adult in their lives who is actively reaching out to them.

If time is limited, you can also use students' preferred mode of communication that they identified during the initial course survey to contact them with a welcome. For students who prefer e-mail, a welcoming e-mail asking for a response may be all that they need. For students who prefer text messages, a quick text message can be sent in almost no time to multiple students. That way students can get your number programmed into their phone and they realize that you're a tech-savvy teacher whom they can text with questions. Never underestimate the power of a text message for a teenager! The average teenager sends 3,339 texts per month (Nielsen Wire, 2010). There's no reason that texting can't be used for their academic as well as their personal communication. Many teens feel most comfortable when texting and they appreciate you adapting your communication style to meet their needs. Finally, for those who prefer a phone call, you can make that five-minute welcome call. That way all your students feel they have been welcomed and you show that you pay attention to their needs and preferences.

Zero Week

As you can see, there's a lot going on in the first week of an online course to build familiarity with the course as well as build relationships. Students are reviewing the syllabus and taking a quiz on it, they are filling out a course survey on which they share their needs and preferences with you, they are participating in a synchronous session from which they get an overview of the course and its tools, and they are having their initial communication with you in a welcome message. These are only the formal assignments that happen during the first week. There are also informal tasks going on such as learning to navigate course tools, trying to figure out the discussion board, trying to get a calendar organized, learning about other students in the class, and so on. To add course content to that workload can be a bit overwhelming. Some teachers, instead, have incorporated the idea of a zero week into their classes. Basically, a zero week is the first week of a course that does not contain much, if any, course content. Instead, zero week is just focused on getting oriented to the class. Following is a sample agenda for zero week:

- Review the course syllabus

- Take a quiz on the syllabus

- Participate in the welcome week webinar

- Complete the initial course survey

- Introduce yourself on the class discussion board and welcome other students to class

- Find someone who shares your interests on the discussion board and strike up a conversation with him or her

In the long run, putting off course content for the first week (or two to three days) won't make a huge impact on your course. You'll still be able to cover the content you need to. However, taking that week off from academic content can make a huge impact on student success. After completing easy tasks in that first week as well as getting to know you and their classmates, students will be far more invested in the class and will truly believe that this is something they can do. Success breeds success and the zero week can be a very strong beginning to an online course.

CONTINUING THE RELATIONSHIP

Once you have used the first weeks of a course to get to know your students, the relationships continue to grow through the purposeful use of course tools. You'll continue to build relationships through discussion boards, announcements, e-mails, and feedback on assignments.

Discussion Boards

There's definitely an art to leading threaded discussions. We'll go into far more detail in chapter 6 on facilitating discussion boards but, for just a moment, let's focus on how discussion boards can be used to build relationships. Consider the discussion board post in the following:

> *Sorry I'm late adding this post. Things have been crazy around here. While reading this section of Hamlet, I was really impressed with how devoted Hamlet is to his father's memory. I'm just not that close to my Dad. He moved away when I was five and we've never really known each other. It's so cool that Hamlet had a dad in his life and cares enough about him to want to preserve his memory, even if it means listening to a ghost!*

As the teacher in this course, there are several ways to respond to this post. One is to create a follow-up post and praise the student for her analysis of Hamlet and his dad. You could also help lead the discussion into what makes a good dad and what evidence we have that Hamlet's father fit the bill. It could be a fascinating discussion built off of one student's personal reaction to the play. Along the way, the student knows that you ''get'' her trouble with her dad and you care about being a positive role model for her. Another way to react might be to call the student and check in. The ''things have been crazy around here'' remark may be a veiled cry for help. It would be a good thing to check in with the student, either via phone or e-mail, and make sure that everything is OK. You will let the student know that you're reading her posts and that you care about her.

Let's consider another post. Read the following post and consider, ''How could I use this discussion post to connect personally with this student and build our relationship?''

> *When we were reading Kipling's poem ''If,'' this week, it made me think about the quarterback controversies in Denver. The poem says ''IF you can keep your head when all about you / Are losing theirs . . . you'll be a Man, my son!'' It made me think of Tebow getting transferred to New York and Cutler getting transferred to Chicago. Tebow totally took it like a man. He kept quiet and, once traded, was really positive about the whole thing. Cutler was a huge baby about the situation, constantly complaining that no one in Denver ever appreciated him. Even though neither situation was fair, according to Kipling Tebow was a man in the situation and Cutler was not.*

In addition to making a really sophisticated connection between a poem and football, this discussion post reveals something about the student. He is an avid football fan, not just following the sport but analyzing trends and reactions of players. This is a real opportunity to connect with the student based on his interest and get to know him better. You could respond to the post and share your Kipling and football connections or you could mention the post in an e-mail to the student.

Either way, the discussion post provides an opportunity for building a relationship with the student based on his or her interests.

Ultimately all discussion posts provide a window to building a relationship with a student. It's critical that instructors take advantage of those opportunities whenever possible.

Announcements

Announcements are yet another opportunity to build relationships with students. In this case, the relationship building is happening because the teacher is using those announcements to say, "I see you!" One easy way to show a student you care is to mention her birthday in an announcement. Something as simple as sharing the week's birthdays and a silly message can help a student feel special. Another way is to give a student or group of students a virtual high five in an announcement when they've done great work. Figure 4.1 shows what that can look like.

Students love being recognized in those announcements and it can go a long way in encouraging them to check in regularly and do a nice job with their work.

E-mails

E-mails are another tool that can be used to build relationships with students. It's not at all uncommon to get e-mails from students such as the following:

Hey Kipp. I'm really behind and starting to panic on what to do. Just wanted to let you know.

There often won't be a signature or even any indication of what the student wanted you to do in order to help. This is just a sign of immaturity and does not necessarily mean that the student is rude. Instead of being frustrated by the student,

Congrats to the group reading 1984! You all did a fantastic job this week having a great discussion and taking your thinking to a deeper level. Well done!

INTERNET
HIGH FIVE
PLACE HAND
HERE

Figure 4.1 Virtual High Five

it's important to view those e-mails as a chance to build a relationship. Here's a possible response:

> *Hi, Jennifer,*
>
> *I'm sorry you're behind. I know the adjustment to online learning can be tough. Can you tell me what's going on and how I can help? Remember that I'm here any time you need help with an assignment or just need to talk out what your priorities should be. Let me know what you need!*
>
> *Btw, I noticed you turned in your poetry assignment. That's a great start. Keep going!*
>
> *Ms. Kipp*

Although it takes longer to write a detailed response to a not-so-detailed initial e-mail, it can go a long way in showing a student that you care. You've also modeled for them what a correct e-mail should look like and asked them to provide you with more information. Over time, the e-mails generally improve and, along the way, you develop a deep relationship with a student, all through electronic text.

Another way that e-mails can build relationships with students is when you initiate the e-mail strand just to say hi or touch base with the student. It's amazing what a response a message like this can get:

> *Hi, Tracy. I just wanted to make sure everything is going OK in class for you. Let me know if you have questions or need help.—Ms. Kipp*

Students often respond with questions or just let me know what's going on in their lives. It's a powerful way to stay connected.

Feedback on Assignments

One of the most surprising places to build relationships with students is in the grading and assessment tools of your LMS. In most systems, every assignment gets submitted to some sort of Dropbox, which is linked to your grade book. When you grade an assignment, the comments you add to the assignment will go directly back to the student in their grades tool. The comments you use there can be powerful ways to improve student performance and build a bridge with a student. Consider the contrast between these two comments on an assignment:

> *Late assignment 75% credit given. Be careful about run-ons in your assignments.*
> *versus*
> *Hi, Tracy. I'm glad you got this in, even if it was late. I noticed that you're still struggling with run-on sentences. Feel free to give me a call or stop by office hours for help with that on the next assignment!*

I've been guilty of providing both types of feedback on my student's work. However, the second option is far more powerful for student learning. First, I used the student's name. It lets the student know that I am focused on his or her personal learning. Second, I praised the student for getting the assignment in. Finally, I identified the problem with the assignment but also suggested ways to improve. That kind of friendly, helpful feedback can really help students feel connected to you and help them want to improve.

All in all, it's important to use a full range of course tools to ensure that you're purposefully building relationships with your students throughout the course.

HOSTING FACE-TO-FACE EVENTS

One other powerful way to build relationships with your students is by hosting face-to-face events as a part of your class. Yes, students come to online learning because they want or need to attend school from home or in a flexible environment. Even so, they still occasionally crave the opportunity to learn face-to-face or at least see each other socially. In my class, students are provided with parent-teacher conferences, back-to-school nights, school mixers, movie nights, and field trips. I don't require students to attend any of these events (because of schedule and location barriers) but they can be a really great way to connect for those students who are able to make it. I find that our relationships are deeper when we at least have some idea of what someone looks like!

My most powerful face-to-face event has been my *Hamlet* movie night. I provide food and a classroom and we watch the Mel Gibson version of *Hamlet*, stopping to discuss throughout. In exchange, students are exempted from one of the assignments in that week's work. I always have great turnout and students love getting to see each other face-to-face. As a bonus, it's a great way to quickly build rapport with kids.

BUILDING AN ONLINE PERSONA

No chapter on building relationships would be complete without a few words about building your online persona. The bottom line is that in an online classroom, for your students, you *are* the text on the screen or the voice in a webinar. Because they have not met you outside of the online course, they have no conception of who you are as a person. You have complete control over the persona you create in that classroom and you have to create that persona thoughtfully and professionally.

I feel that part of my role as an online teacher is to serve as a translator between my physical self and my electronic self. If you are the funny teacher who told a lot of jokes in a face-to-face classroom, you need to find ways to be that person in your online classroom. Maybe you post comic strips in the announcements or take time out for storytelling during webinars. Or if you are the passionate teacher who challenges students to care about history, not just learn it, you need to find a way to be that person in your online classroom. Maybe you share your passion in the discussion board with prompts that constantly connect history to present day or maybe you post current events to the announcements to start a discussion. It's only when you become a real person to your students that they can have a relationship with you and care about your class.

Interview with Steven Sproles, Virtual Virginia

Steven Sproles is a teacher with Virtual Virginia, a state-led virtual school program. Each semester he teaches approximately seventy-five students in economics and personal finance courses. Sproles says that the greatest thing about teaching online is that he gets to spend less time on managing a classroom and more time interacting with kids. In fact, Sproles feels like he spends more time in academic interactions with students than he ever did in the past because he doesn't have to keep "reinventing the wheel" on content. Once he's created a video on a particular topic, it's there for all future semesters and he can focus on helping students instead of delivering that lecture again.

He often starts the day by sending out an instant message to all his students. They'll receive the message as they log in and he'll get messages back from them all day. Something as simple as, "How was your weekend?" can elicit a lot of responses and help students know he cares. Sproles also uses podcasts and quick recordings via Wimba, a webinar tool, to share content with students and help reteach a concept when they're not getting it.

With all those interactions throughout the day, it can be difficult to keep track of all his student's needs. To help cope, Sproles keeps a cheat sheet where he records information on different students' interests. If a student mentions that he plays soccer, Sproles will write it down on a spreadsheet and remember to ask the student how it's going the next time they interact. Students really appreciate that he takes the time to get to know them and those interactions clearly demonstrate that Sproles cares.

Sproles's greatest piece of advice for new online teachers is, "don't be afraid to explore and find out what works." He admits that he doesn't have it all figured out but he's happy to tweak things and constantly make the learning experience better for kids!

FOCUS ON BLENDED LEARNING

One of the great advantages to working in a blended environment is that relationships can be developed at a much quicker pace than in courses that are solely online. The time a class has together in a physical classroom can be great for building rapport and a classroom culture. You'll want to make sure you take a class period or two early in the course to establish expectations and build relationships when you're all together in the same physical space. That way conversations and collaboration in the online environment can flourish, having already laid a foundation for success while inside a traditional classroom.

CHAPTER FIVE

USING ANNOUNCEMENTS EFFECTIVELY

ESSENTIAL QUESTIONS:

- What kinds of announcements should be on the main page of a course?

- How can I use announcements to connect with my students?

- How often should I post announcements and what content should they contain?

- How can I enrich my announcements with images, humor, and formatting?

- How can I include voice elements within announcements?

One of the most important tools in your LMS is your announcements area. Sometimes you'll also see this area called the *updates tool*. The announcements area is a space you can use to communicate important messages to your class. Most often, it's the landing page for when students log in to your class. Before they see any other content, they see your announcements area.

In a face-to-face classroom, this tool is the equivalent of the bulletin board and whiteboard that are often at the front of the room. It's a place to remind students of upcoming due dates, keep a running list of announcements, pin important tidbits from the school, and so on.

Because the announcements area is the first thing that students will see of your classroom on a daily basis, it's very important to make sure that it is a well-organized, welcoming, and also an interactive space. As with all the communication areas of your course, you want students to feel connected to the course and to you. The announcements area can be an excellent space to do that.

TYPES OF ANNOUNCEMENTS

At any one time, students in your courses will see approximately three to four different announcements on the main announcements page of your course. Those announcements will fall into six basic categories: weekly announcements, due date reminders, special bulletins, current events, way-to-go, and social announcements. In my course, I try to keep just one weekly announcement on the main page. All other announcements fall into one of the other five categories. Let's explore what these announcement types are and how you can use them in your course.

Weekly Announcements

The first type of announcement is the weekly announcement. The weekly announcement is really a road map for what you're doing in the course and where you're headed next. It lets students know what they should currently be working on and when that work is due. You can expect that students will be referring to the weekly announcement on a regular basis.

Weekly announcements should contain several key pieces of information:

- An overview of the content to be studied in the upcoming week. This is just a one to two sentence mention of the content to be studied that week and why students should care about that content. Along with the overview, there should be a content-related image that can help students connect to what's happening in that session. For example, my students recently completed a unit where they were watching a YouTube video of The Beatles performing a portion of *A Midsummer Night's Dream* and then critically analyzing their performance. My announcement for that week said, ''Welcome to a new week in English 10! This week we'll consider how actors can affect the interpretation of a play. In this case, the actors we'll be studying are The Beatles!'' Then, next to that overview, I had a crazy picture of The Beatles performing the play. The image gave students a connection to the content for that week but also got them interested in where we were heading as a class.

- Information about which session students should be working on in the upcoming week. This is more than simply saying that everyone should be working on Unit 3 Session 5. I try to always give my students a to-do list of what's in that session and how many points each of those assignments will be worth. Putting that information into a simple table can help students conceptualize the work as well as know when they are near the end of the session (and how much time they may need to allow for that week's work).

- Heads-up announcements about upcoming items on the calendar or important things that are going on in the school. This might include announcements as varied as information about an upcoming field trip or information about how to turn in late work. When I taught face-to-face, I always tried to repeat information three or four times to make sure every student heard it. Teaching online is no different. I want students to see a piece of information via announcements, e-mail, and live sessions, at a minimum. The heads-up announcements are just another place to share important information with them.

- A suggested schedule, especially if your students are moving through the course together as a cohort. The suggested schedule takes the full week's worth of work (usually a single session) and breaks it down by day. So, if I were going to complete Unit 3 Session 5 in one week, here's what I would do on Monday, Tuesday, Wednesday, Thursday, and Friday. Teenagers usually struggle with time management. Providing them with a weekly schedule is an easy way to scaffold their transition into online learning and into adultlike time management. At the beginning of second semester, I usually ask my returning students to give some advice to the new students about how to be successful in my course. They consistently say that new students should follow the suggested schedule because it's the best way to keep up with the work in class.

Once you've put all this information together, the weekly announcement might take up to ten inches of screen real estate on your main page. It also should live on the main page for at least a week, providing critical direction to students about how they should be proceeding with their schoolwork. It's worth the space because the content is so important.

Figure 5.1 is an example of a weekly announcement and what it could look like in your course.

You can see how this announcement gives students all the information that they need in a visually pleasing format that's easy to reference when they have questions. Providing the information one week at a time means that students always know where we're headed and how we're getting there.

Wednesday April 25–Tuesday May 1

Welcome to a new week in English 10 and to a new unit! This is the last unit of the year! This unit is focused on an author study. We'll be reading and examining the work of John Steinbeck. *Be sure you have a copy of your novel for this unit!*

Unit 10 Session 1 will be due Tuesday, May 1, before midnight.

We will have a live session this Wednesday, April 25, at 3:30 pm.

Important Announcements:

-Grades: If you're struggling, please contact Ms Kipp. ASAP. I can work with you to get you up to passing!

-Steinbeck novel: You need a copy of your Steinbeck novel starting immediately! You may choose from *Of Mice and Men, The Pearl, The Red Pony, Tortilla Flat,* or *Cannery Row.* All are available at the public library or in used and new bookstores.

To do by Tuesday, May 1, before midnight:

Unit 10 Session 1	Point Value
Steinbeck background assignment	30 points
Author's ideas discussion	15 points
Total points	**45 points**

Suggested Schedule*:

Wed 4/25	Thurs 4/26	Fri 4/27		Mon 4/30	Tues 5/1
Watch Steinbeck video and keep list of events, and then submit.

Attend live session or watch the recording. | Read Steinbeck letter.

Make initial post to the writing ideas discussion board. | Make at least two more posts to the writing ideas discussion board.

Begin reading the first quarter of your Steinbeck novel. | W e e k e n d | Continue reading the first quarter of your Steinbeck novel. | Finish reading the first quarter of your Steinbeck novel. |

*Note that weeks in this course usually run from Wednesday to Tuesday. New work appears on Wednesday and it's due the following Tuesday.

Let me know if you have any questions. I'm here to help!

Ms. Kipp

Figure 5.1 Sample Weekly Announcement

Note: If your LMS system doesn't allow for a lengthy announcement such as this one, an alternative would be to create a full page of content within each session that includes this information. Then, your announcement page can be linked to that lengthier page with the content you need to communicate to students.

Due Date Reminders

Unlike the weekly announcement, the rest of the announcement types mentioned are all much shorter. They should take up no more than three to four inches of screen real estate, maximum, and they should only appear for two to three days on the main page; otherwise, the main page can get too cluttered.

The first of the more minor announcement types is a due date reminder. Although students can see the assignment due dates in multiple places including in e-mails, the course calendar, live sessions, and the weekly announcement, sometimes it can be helpful to reinforce a due date one more time via a due date reminder announcement, especially if the assignment is a large one and you notice that much of the class is falling behind. This announcement just gives students a heads-up that they have a major project due.

Figure 5.2 is an example of a due date reminder. The most important announcements also usually have red titles. The color is a great signal to students that this is something they don't want to miss!

Special Bulletins

Another of the more minor announcement types is a special bulletin. Formatted much like a due date reminder, these announcements are for critical changes in policy or for major upcoming school events. I've used special bulletin announcements when I need students to register for a test or if I need to change a due date in the course. Similar to a due date reminder announcement, I try to use a red header on these announcements to signal to students that the content is especially

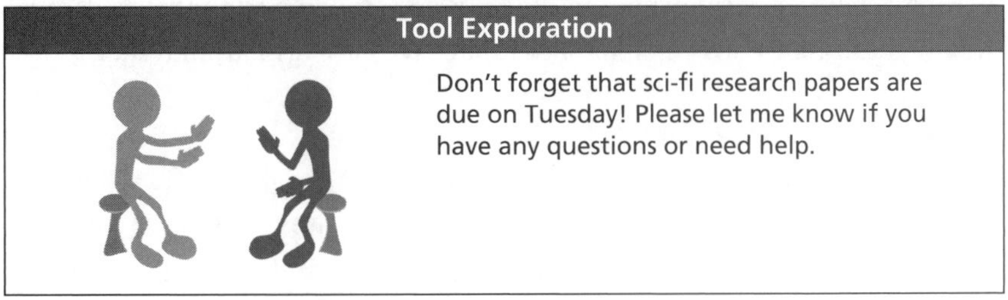

Tool Exploration

Don't forget that sci-fi research papers are due on Tuesday! Please let me know if you have any questions or need help.

Figure 5.2 Sample Due Date Reminder

Figure 5.3   Sample Current Event Announcement

important. As much as possible, I try to minimize special bulletin announcements and only use them for absolutely critical issues.

Current Events

Unlike the other minor announcement types, a current event announcement is not related to the core content of the course. It's an announcement that you use to share interesting information about your subject and how it's related to current events in the world. Students need to know that your subject is relevant and timely. What better way to share that than to direct them to an article that relates to something you've been discussing in class. I try to keep a running list of interesting articles and post a current event announcement every couple of weeks. Sometimes I will incorporate an extra credit opportunity into the current event announcement but most often I just share it with students as an interesting tidbit. Figure 5.3 is an example.

Through these current event announcements, students are exposed to my subject area in addition to how that subject relates to the world around them.

Way-to-Go Announcements

Another minor announcement type I try to use on a regular basis is the way-to-go announcement. These announcements are an opportunity to brag about students who are doing an exceptional job. It could be that a student made a particularly insightful discussion post and you want to make sure everyone reads it. Or it could be that a group of students did a really nice job with their wiki and you want to highlight their work, maybe even sharing the link. Going even larger scale, it could be that you were impressed with how the entire class did on a particular assignment and want to give them all kudos. No matter how large the group you want to recognize, everyone loves getting positive accolades. The announcements area can be a great space to give well-deserving students a pat on the back.

Before moving on from this point, I do want to mention a word of warning about way-to-go announcements. Although it's really important to give students positive feedback, you do have to be careful to maintain confidentiality. When you're praising a student, be careful to never mention their actual grade in the post because that information is private. Even so, you can say that someone did a good job on an assignment without sharing the grade.

Social Announcements

The final announcement type that you'll want to consider using in your class is the social announcement. These are announcements that are not content related but are focused on particular students and events going on in their lives, such as celebrating a student's birthday or saying good luck to a student participating in a play. When you can, it's great to include an image of the student for further engagement. Every student enjoys seeing their name highlighted and it's another way to keep kids connected with each other and with the class.

PRACTICAL CONSIDERATIONS IN USING ANNOUNCEMENTS

Now that you have an understanding of the types of content that you can include in an announcement, let's spend a few moments thinking about practical tips for how you share that content.

How Often to Post Announcements

There's definitely a critical balance when you consider how often you should be posting announcements to your course. On the one hand, you don't want to have to post an announcement every day. For one thing, that's an unnecessary time commitment. For another, you won't have important information to post every day and you want to use the announcements for only the most critical information. On the other hand, you don't want your announcements area to become so stagnant that students don't check it. If the same announcement is there every day for two weeks, they'll stop looking for a new announcement and just breeze through the announcements page.

In general, a good rule of thumb is to add some sort of announcement every two to three days. That way the announcements change often enough to keep the attention of your students but don't change so often that they become meaningless. You want to maintain the integrity of the announcements area and make sure that everyone gets all the information they need.

Considering Your Tone in Announcements

As in all areas of your course, your announcements area should maintain a friendly, professional tone. Once you've written an announcement, you'll want to read it through a few times to make sure that it's factually accurate and grammatically correct as well as pleasant to read. In the beginning, this will feel like a lot of work but it's worth it to maintain the quality of your course. Students should feel like you're having a personal conversation with them about the course as they read through your announcements. That means that your tone must be professional but also excited and fun. As you've seen in the previous examples, I tend to overuse exclamation points. I want students to know that I'm excited about this course and about their progress in it and I tend to rely on exclamation points to convey that enthusiasm. The only way you'll achieve the sort of tone you're aiming for is very careful reading and very careful writing. Students will appreciate your attention to detail and your positive communications.

Using Humor

Along with a friendly tone, you'll also want to explore the possibility of including humor in your announcements. We learn better when we're relaxed and humor is a great way to make connections with students and help them feel comfortable in your class space. One way to include humor is through your images. Cartoons and funny pictures can be a great way to break the ice in an announcement. You can also consider using sarcasm in some of your announcements and even telling jokes. Students need to know that you're a real person who laughs in addition to grading papers all day!

Although humor is a very effective teaching tool, it also needs to be used with caution. Sometimes written text won't convey your sense of humor as easily as sharing a joke with someone in person, especially in the case of sarcasm. For example, you might say to a student in person, ''You need an extension *again*! Do you *ever* meet a deadline?'' and the student would understand that you're joking because of the tone of your voice. They'd still feel supported and cared for. However, in writing, the sarcasm simply doesn't translate, especially if students don't understand how italics can help convey emphasis in a sentence. As a teacher, you'll either have to tone down your sarcasm with students or use emoticons to indicate to a student that you're joking. As in the previous example, a winking emoticon,;-), will tell a student that you're joking. Even so, it's wise to be cautious so you don't offend your students.

Making Your Announcements Visually Appealing

You'll also want to take some time to make your announcements as visually appealing as possible. You may have noticed that I use a basic template in most of my announcements to keep the look consistent and visually appealing. The template is a basic table in a word processing document with a colored header, a space for an image, and a space for text. Then I make the borders invisible. I save that file and open it any time I want to add an announcement or a content page to my course. That way the template is always ready.

Another key element in making your announcements visually appealing is to include images whenever possible. We are visual beings and having an image to connect to an idea makes the idea easier to remember. Then, when students revisit the announcements page, they don't have to read every announcement to remember what it said. They can simply scan the images and those images will help them remember what they need to know. Many schools have a set of stock images just for this purpose. If not, the royalty-free site Stock.xchng is a great source for free images (http://sxc.hu). Google Images is another option. Eye-catching images help make great, engaging announcements; however, you will need to be careful to not infringe on copyright.

Keeping Your Home Page Clean

As mentioned previously, when students log into a course, they should never see more than three to four announcements on the main page. Otherwise the space becomes visually cluttered and students aren't sure how far down the page they really need to read. It will be up to you as the facilitator of the course to clean out the announcements page on a regular basis and keep it neat for your students. There are a few things you can do to make that task more manageable.

One way to keep your main page clean is to create an announcement archive somewhere in your course. I like to have mine in my course info section along with my syllabus. This is just a folder where I can copy and paste old announcements that have expired from the main page. Then, if students are working behind in the course or need to find an old announcement, they always have a space to refer back to. The last announcement on my page directs students to the announcement archive so they can find an announcement that is no longer living on the main page.

Another thing you can do to keep your main page clean is to make good use of the adaptive release feature in your LMS, which allows you to set a time when the announcement should appear as well as an expiration date. I like to have them appear at 12:01 A.M. on the day that the announcement is applicable. Weekly announcements can be set to expire as soon as the due date they refer to has passed. The same is true for the minor announcements. That way, even if you forget to come back and manually move the announcement to the archive, it still disappears for students and keeps the main announcement page clean.

INCORPORATING VOICE ELEMENTS INTO ANNOUNCEMENTS

Once you have mastered the basic content of your regular announcements, you may find that you want to begin experimenting with adding your actual voice to your announcements page. Again, students want to know that you're a real person and hearing your voice can go a long way in personalizing your instruction.

One of the easiest ways to add your voice to an announcement is to make a recording of yourself using the microphone on your computer. Then embed the file within an announcement along with a player on the screen. Students can hit play and hear you explain the announcement in addition to reading it on the screen. This is a fantastic modification for oral learners. Audacity is a free tool for making those voice recordings and most LMSs have a player function built in when you attach an mp3 to an announcement. Many LMSs also have built in tools that will allow you to record your voice and easily embed it on an announcement without having to use a separate program. These are great options to explore and well worth your time.

Another way you can include your voice in an announcement is to use a tool like Voki. Voki creates a digital avatar that you can embed on any web page. It combines a recorded voice message with your avatar that will move its mouth to match your words. I've used a snowman avatar to tell students about upcoming winter break and an alien avatar to let students know about our upcoming sci-fi unit. I've also used a normal, human avatar when I'm telling the students something more serious. The kids love seeing your creativity while also getting to hear your voice.

Overall, the announcements tool is one of the most powerful tools in your arsenal. It's a space to help students connect to your content and also keeps them focused and headed in the right direction. By following a few simple rules, you can help make that space as efficient and effective as possible.

FOCUS ON BLENDED LEARNING

In a blended course, it can be tempting to completely skip making announcements to the class via the LMS and instead make all announcements in the face-to-face portion of your course. However, in doing that you may be handicapping your communications with students. Some students simply don't (or won't!) listen well in a classroom. After they get home to complete their online course work, they may find themselves saying, ''Now wait, what was I supposed to do?'' If you've posted those directions in the announcements portion of your course, you'll save yourself some time and save your students from some frustrations. They can always double check the announcements to make sure they're working on the right content.

CHAPTER SIX

DISCUSSION BOARD STRATEGIES AND FACILITATION

ESSENTIAL QUESTIONS:

- What kinds of questions lend themselves well to discussion board posts?

- How do I grade an online discussion?

- How can I take discussions deeper?

- What is my role in an online discussion?

- How can students help facilitate a discussion board?

- How should I react when students ''misbehave'' in an online discussion?

In some ways, facilitating an online discussion board is the most foreign thing that a new online teacher will do. A written discussion held over the course of several days bears little in common with a verbal discussion held in a forty-five-minute class period. However, in at least three core ways, online discussions can actually be superior to traditional verbal discussions.

- An online discussion is not bound by a class period or a bell. Ideas are allowed to grow over the course of several days or perhaps even several weeks. Instead of an idea being mentioned by one person and then dropped in favor of the topic most interesting to the class, a pair of students can elaborate on an idea within their own space and the rest of the students move on to other ideas that they find interesting. There are far fewer lost ideas that just never have the time to grow and flourish. Instead of a topic dying with the end of a class period, that topic can be revisited during the course of time as student's ideas on a topic mature and fluctuate. Discussions are in fact deeper and richer because they have time to grow.

- An online discussion requires participation by all members of the class. Face-to-face discussions are often dominated by those who are the loudest or speak for the longest period of time. Shy, quiet, or slow students are censored in favor of those who are better equipped to speak quickly (or loudly). That's not so in an online discussion. Shy students, working in an online discussion board, are able to develop their voices. They're able to form their thoughts, revise them, and finally share them in the class forum. It's a beautiful thing to see a shy student challenge an outgoing student to a lively debate, all without intimidation!

- Online discussions are recorded and easily graded. I always struggled with grading an in-class discussion. How could you say who had the most valid ideas and who participated well? Everything happens so fast! I usually resorted to a tally system and just marked down when students participated. If a statement was unusually insightful, a student might get two tallies instead of just one. Five tallies equals 100 percent, four tallies equals 90 percent, and so on. To be honest, it was a lousy way to grade a discussion but it was the best method I had. All that changes in the online discussion board. Every student's comments are recorded for my viewing. I can see exactly what was said, by whom, when, and about what. I can easily see how many times a student contributed to a discussion and the quality of those posts. In most systems, I can even see the average number of words per post and how often those posts generated further discussions! Assessment of an online discussion is not only simpler but it's more valid in assessing students' understanding of the topic and their ability to discuss that topic with their peers.

Clearly the online discussion board has several qualities that make it superior to a traditional discussion. However, when not done well, it can also be a painful experience for students as well as the teacher. In this chapter, we'll explore online discussions and how to make them a successful experience in your course.

DISCUSSION BOARD BASICS

First, let's start with the basics. What is a discussion board? Different LMSs call this tool by different names. You might see it called a *forum, discussion board, update feed*, or *threaded discussion*. For simplicity, I'll use the term *discussion board* or *discussion tool* throughout this chapter. Put at its simplest, the discussion tool provides a space for students to respond to a prompt shared by the teacher. Then, once students have responded to the initial prompt, the discussion tool gives students the opportunity to respond to each other's posts and keep the discussion moving deeper. Figure 6.1 shows an example of a discussion tool in the Blackboard LMS.

You can see how each post can build on the last and develop a really in-depth discussion around a particular idea.

Figure 6.2 shows the discussion tool in the Schoology LMS.

Although the tools look a little different, they accomplish the same purpose: students are able to create an in-depth discussion on a content-related question.

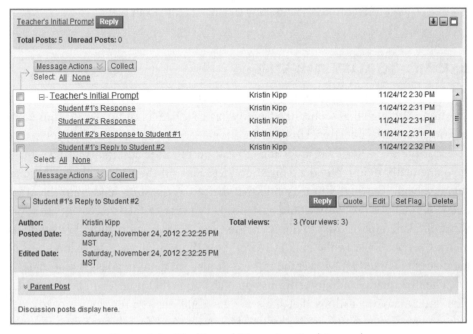

Figure 6.1 Blackboard Discussion Tool Example

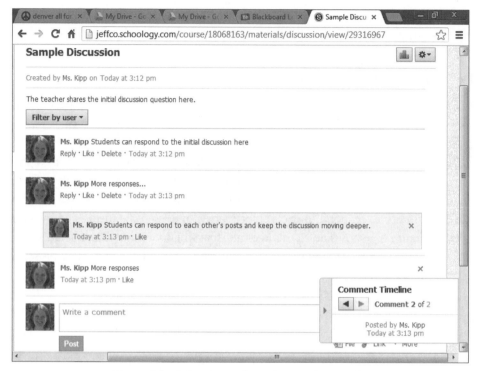

Figure 6.2 Schoology Discussion Tool Example

ASKING QUALITY QUESTIONS

The first step in creating a good online discussion is to start with an interesting question. Although that seems like a pretty basic skill, a lot of finesse is required in creating that initial question. Unlike a traditional face-to-face discussion, you won't necessarily have a series of questions to ask during a discussion. Instead, you'll have one really rich, really deep question that kicks off the entire debate. Then, as students begin posting, you may find that the initial question leads into the other questions that you probably would have posed in a face-to-face discussion. In some ways, it takes a lot of trust to allow the discussion to develop and allow students to ask the questions. In the end, however, you'll find that the discussion goes all the places you would have wanted it to go. It just got there in a less direct route!

The first quality of a good discussion question is that it needs to be debatable. You should save questions that have a clear right answer for your quizzes and assignments. Discussions, instead, should focus on ideas for which there is no right answer. The goal is to create critical thinkers who can reason through some of the great debates within your subject area and, to that end, your questions should challenge their thinking, not just their basic knowledge.

The second quality of a good discussion question is that it should only be *one* question. As teachers, we are so often tempted to include a compound question with multiple facets and goat trails. Too often, a student looks at a question like that and has no idea what it's asking because it's too complicated. Your questions should be relatively straightforward and directly related to the content you've been studying. If you find that you simply have too many questions to ask for a particular topic, as an alternative you can provide four or five prompts for a discussion and ask students to respond to one of them. That way a student's response should still remain focused on a single idea but the class discussion overall will focus on all the topics that you were hoping for. Rest assured that as the discussion facilitator you can guide the discussion into multiple avenues as well through your posts. The discussion question itself doesn't have to do all the work. It simply needs to get the discussion started.

Finally, a good discussion question should ask students to provide evidence. There's nothing worse than an adult who has lots of opinions but no facts! Your questions as well as your grading should value providing evidence in any response.

Following are a few example questions in different subject areas. As you review them, think about different discussion questions you could create for your content area:

English: In your reading this week, you reviewed a letter by Steinbeck stating that there are no rules for a good short story. Do you agree with his opinion? Why or why not?

Social studies: How would the world be different if Germany had won World War II rather than the Allies?

Math: Some people have argued that because of calculators, students should no longer have to memorize addition facts or multiplication tables. Do you agree? What impact would not memorizing those facts have on your understanding of math or the speed with which you complete math problems?

Science: Do you think the scientific method creates more creative thinkers? How is creativity necessary to scientific exploration?

Economics: In the last twenty-four hours, what opportunity costs have you had to pay because you were working in your online courses? What benefits will you gain from having given up those opportunities? If you were to conduct a cost-benefit analysis for schoolwork, what might it look like?

Study skills: This semester we have talked at great length about goal setting and how it can affect your future success. What goals did you set at the beginning of the semester and have you found those goals to be motivating?

Journalism: Journalists have gone to jail in the past for protecting their sources. Why is protecting sources important to a journalist's credibility? Is it worth going to jail in order to protect a source?

RUBRICS AND GRADING

Once you've ensured that you're asking good questions in your online discussion board and you've held your first student discussion, the challenge becomes how to assess students' participation within that discussion board. This is definitely a situation in which you get what you measure. You'll want to set clear expectations for student participation in the discussion board and then consistently evaluate student work based on those expectations.

In general, discussion board rubrics have at least three categories for assessing students:

- *The number of discussion posts.* For each discussion, you'll want to set a minimum number of posts that a student should add and a final deadline for those posts. For my class, students are generally asked to respond three to four times per discussion, once as an initial post in which they respond to my prompt. Then the other posts are all in response to other students' posts. I tell students that only substantial posts will be counted in their overall total number. Substantial posts are those that keep the discussion moving by expanding on an idea or asking a question. Posts that simply repeat the content of another post or simply say, ''I agree'' or ''good job'' don't count in a student's overall number.

- *The quality of the posts.* Posts that show critical thinking, expand on the ideas of another student, or refer to outside resources generally receive full credit. Posts that are not substantial may receive partial credit or no credit at all. Please note that if you're only counting substantial posts in the overall number of posts for your quantity category, you may not need a category for the quality of the posts.

- *The timing of the posts and discussion board etiquette.* This category encourages students to make their initial post early in the week (perhaps by day three of a seven-day week) and then make follow-up posts regularly rather than waiting until the last minute. It's very difficult to have a quality discussion if all the students are posting on the day a discussion is due. The discussion doesn't have time to develop and students who try to post early in the week are frustrated by a lack of participation. You'll also want to include information within this category about discussion board etiquette. Students who regularly ask questions of other students and draw out deeper answers from others should be rewarded in their grades.

Exhibits 6.1 through 6.3 show three examples of discussion board rubrics. Exhibit 6.1 is a holistic rubric, which will work best if your LMS only gives you a small space to respond to student work. Exhibit 6.2 is a rubric that shows each rubric category outlined with a point value for the discussion. This rubric will work best in LMSs in which you can attach a rubric to each discussion and complete it easily. Exhibit 6.3 is a rubric that focuses only on the number of total posts, with only substantial posts counted.

Exhibit 6.1. Holistic Rubric

9–10 points, Exemplary response	Student responded at least four times in the discussion. Discussion posts are spread throughout the week with at least one post by Wednesday. Each discussion post is of high quality and shows critical thinking. At least some posts provide evidence or quotations to support opinions. Student consistently takes the discussion deeper and asks questions to keep the discussion moving.
8 points, Good response	Student responded at least three times to the discussion with posts spread throughout the week. Most discussion posts are of high quality. At least one post asks a question to keep the discussion moving.

(continued)

Exhibit 6.1. Holistic Rubric (*continued*)

6–7 points, Fair response	Student responded at least two times to the discussion. Posts are of average quality. Future posts should focus on taking the discussion deeper or asking questions to keep the discussion moving. Also remember to respond in the discussion board throughout the week.
< 5 points, Unacceptable response	Student did not post to the discussion board more than once or responses were of poor quality. Future attempts should focus on meeting the minimum number of required posts and making sure that each post is of high quality.

Exhibit 6.2. Detailed Rubric

	Exemplary	Good	Fair	Unacceptable
Number of posts	Four or more discussion posts	Three or more discussion posts	Two or more discussion posts	Fewer than two discussion posts

	Exemplary	Good	Fair	Unacceptable
Quality of posts	Discussion posts show critical thinking and clearly address the prompt. Evidence is included to support all opinions. Outside sources are referenced when appropriate.	Discussion posts clearly address the prompt. Ideas are developed fully and often include evidence.	Discussion posts address the prompt but may not be fully developed or supported.	Discussion posts are off topic or don't add significantly to the discussion.
Timing and etiquette	Discussion posts are spread throughout the week with the first post by mid-week. Responses to other students are respectful and help the student to clarify their thinking.	Discussion posts are spread throughout the week. Responses to other students are respectful.	Discussion posts may not be spread throughout the week. Responses to other students are respectful but may not take the discussion deeper.	Discussion posts were made all in one day or responses to other students were simply paraphrases that did not take the discussion deeper.

Exhibit 6.3. Rubric Based on Number of Substantial Posts

Definition of a substantial post: A substantial post clearly responds to the topic in the prompt. It includes specific evidence, quotations, or outside resources to support opinions. If the post is in response to another student, it clearly builds on one of the ideas in the original post or asks a clarifying question that keeps the discussion moving.

4 substantial posts: 10 points

3 substantial posts: 8 points

2 substantial posts: 7 points

1 substantial post: 6 points

0 substantial posts: 0 points

Each of these discussion board rubrics has strengths and weaknesses. You'll want to choose and modify the one that best fits your teaching style as well as the strengths of your LMS.

You'll also want to think through a policy for late discussion posts. In my classroom, I don't give credit for late discussions. I tell students that coming to a discussion late is like walking into a face-to-face classroom after everyone has left and sharing your ideas. Because no one is there to hear you, your contributions aren't adding anything to the overall class experience. Therefore, I don't give credit for them. Students learn very quickly to get discussion posts in on time and that discussions are a valuable part of our learning experience.

TEACHING STUDENTS TO RESPOND IN WAYS THAT KEEP THE DISCUSSION MOVING

One of the pitfalls of an online discussion is when students are posting to the discussion the required number of posts but their discussion posts do not keep the discussion moving or add to it. Thus, the discussion stalls on a series of stale answers. Students get bored because there's nothing new in the discussion and the ideas are not stimulating. There are a few ways to avoid this or correct it.

First, it's absolutely vital, as discussed previously, to explain to students the kind of response you're looking for. Share examples of really great discussion posts and, when you find those kinds of posts in a discussion, don't be afraid to praise the student publicly so other students see what you're looking for.

Second, when you see a student consistently providing poor answers or answers that stall out the discussion, it's your job as the facilitator to communicate that with the student privately. An e-mail, text message, or phone call can go a long way in letting students know that you're reading their posts and that there's room for improvement.

Finally, if you see a discussion beginning to stall, you can intervene as the facilitator. Ask a new question, redirect the core ideas, or expand on the stalled idea in a new way. Students depend on you as the responsible adult in the class to intervene when you need to and to keep the discussions as high quality as possible. The following is an example dialogue that demonstrates how a teacher can redirect a conversation to deepen it or keep it moving:

Initial prompt: In what ways is the scientific method important to the advancement of new ideas in science?

Student 1: Well, without the scientific method we wouldn't know which ideas work and which ones don't. We'd have a bunch of people just throwing ideas out there to see what people might like.

Student 2: There are a lot of dumb ideas out there. The scientific method helps scientists sort out the dumb ones.

Student 3: I agree with both of you. The scientific method is important. (The conversation has stalled at this point. Students are simply repeating the ideas shared by others and not adding anything new. It's time for the teacher to intervene.)

Teacher: I recently read a blog proposing that no one should vaccinate their children because vaccines aren't that effective. How could we apply the scientific method to this situation to prove or disprove the new idea? How would the scientific method be important to future science in this area?

By intervening in this discussion, the teacher has taken a potentially dull conversation and made it more practical, helping students to apply their ideas in a real-world situation. Although the conversation might get sidetracked into a discussion of vaccines, it will also be an interesting application of the scientific method and demonstrate why the method is so important to the future of science.

Basic redirection and questioning is a critical skill of a quality online teacher. If you need some practice, check out an online discussion board for a topic of your choice. There are boards out there for everything from gardening to model railroads. They're full of interesting conversations that can help you develop your skills as a facilitator.

When all else fails, you can also encourage high-quality posts with rigorous grading. It's one thing to share a rubric with students. It's another thing to apply it consistently in a way that changes behavior. If students are not living up to your expectations, teach them how to meet those expectations and grade accordingly.

TEACHING DISCUSSION BOARD ETIQUETTE

Before your first discussion, you'll want to be sure that you teach students a few basic etiquette rules for discussion boards. You want students to remember that they are dealing with real people in these discussions and that disrespectful posts will not be tolerated. A safe learning environment is just as important in an online classroom as it is in a face-to-face classroom. Here are a few etiquette rules to share with students:

- Remember that these are real people you're having a discussion with. If you wouldn't say something to a person in real life, don't say it to them in our discussion forums.

- Never type in all caps. That's considered shouting and it's very rude!

- If you need to disagree with someone's idea, do it in a respectful way. Explain why you think differently and provide evidence for your opinion.

- When a particular discussion thread changes topics drastically from the original student's post, change the title of the thread so that other students can see that the subject has shifted. That way they won't waste their time looking for a particular topic they were interested in, based on the subject line, only to find that you're talking about something different.

- Make your initial post early in the week so that there are lots of opportunities for other students to respond to your great ideas!

As with students who need to improve the quality of their posts, students who break etiquette rules should be corrected privately via e-mail, text, or a phone call. Most of the time students are not being intentionally rude. They just need a caring adult to show them a better way to respond.

One of the best ways to teach your etiquette rules is to model them yourself. When you're respectfully guiding the discussion and taking a student's learning deeper, other students will see that and learn how to do it themselves based on your example.

HOW MUCH TO BE INVOLVED

There's definitely a fine balance when thinking about the teacher's role in an online discussion. As the facilitator of a discussion, your job is to facilitate but that can too easily fall into taking over a discussion. The last thing you want to do is find yourself leading every discussion, on every topic, with students having no ownership of the process. However, you don't want to be completely absent from a discussion either. In the absence of a teacher, discussions tend to stay at surface level and may never get to the meatier content that you really want students to explore. Your job is to find a balance between taking over and being absent.

As a general rule of thumb, I try to post about four to five times per discussion, just like my students. In that way, I'm not taking over a discussion but I'm also not completely absent from it. Because I limit myself on the total number of posts, I try to make every one of those posts count. Every time I post, it's for a specific purpose. It may be that a discussion has gone stale and students need a new direction to explore in their ideas. It may be that a particular group of students has forgotten to provide evidence and I need to encourage critical thinking in those responses. It may be that a discussion has gone off on a goat trail and I need to redirect it to a core idea. It may be that a particular student has made a really strong insight and I want to praise it and go deeper. No matter why I'm posting, I always have a purpose for a particular post. If I find myself typing a response to a post but it doesn't seem to be of critical importance once I have it drafted, I delete the post and move on to the next student response. I want every response I add to the discussion to be interesting and purposeful so that students will look for my comments and know that their time will be well spent!

TYPES OF POSTS

In addition to ensuring that my posts to a discussion are purposeful, I also try to include at least one landscape post and one summary post in each discussion. These are powerful templates for posts that will improve a discussion and take it deeper.

The landscape post is a template for a discussion post that I learned from a PBS Teacherline course ("Online Facilitator Training I: Mastering the Skills of Online Teaching"). This post is something you use in the middle of a discussion to provide the lay of the land from the discussion so far. It quotes two or three students from earlier in the discussion and shows how their ideas are related to or in contrast to each other. Then it takes those ideas and encourages students to take the idea deeper. Because students are quoted by name, it can be a great way to reward good posts but it can also encourage the rest of the class to take a closer look at those posts. Here's an example of a landscape post:

> So far it sounds like we have really contrasting views of the writing process and how a person learns to write. Nick says that "writing is a mystery that I've never really been able to figure out. Sometimes I sit down to write and it's really good. Other times it's awful. . . ." while Brittany says, "I used to think that writing was a talent that you couldn't learn but then I had a really good seventh-grade English teacher who taught me a process that really works for me. My writing's still not great but it's better." Do you have a process that works for you when you write? Do you think all good writers need to have a process?

The post clearly shows students where the discussion has been going and then points it in a new direction. It can be a really great way to redirect a discussion, keep it moving, and also reward some great student work.

Another type of post you'll want to include is a summary or wrap-up post. Many facilitators include this post in a discussion board itself but others put it in the course announcements. The summary post, similar to a landscape post, can also quote particular students but the core purpose is to give a discussion a sense of closure. It should summarize the core ideas from the discussion and then help connect that content to what's coming next in the course. Here's an example:

> In this week's discussion we shared some really interesting ideas about how the world would be different if Germany had won World War II. Some of you pointed out that the United States would no longer be a world power and probably wouldn't even exist anymore. Hitler intended to take over all of Europe and probably would not have stopped there. Others pointed out that our culture would be very different. Nazi Germany valued conformity in races and in opinions. Multiculturalism would not be valued and we would have lost much of our diversity. Then, there's the obvious point that we might all be speaking German! I think we can all be glad that the Allied forces prevailed and won the war. In next week's session, we'll look at the rebuilding of Germany and how those cultural values that helped create the Nazi party had to change drastically in order to provide for a new German state.

As you can see, the summary post provides a nice sense of continuity for a course and helps students see how a particular discussion is connected to the overall flow of a course.

HANDING OVER THE REINS FOR STUDENT-LED DISCUSSIONS

Once you have discussions running smoothly in your online classroom, you'll also want to explore the possibility of having students facilitate discussions on their own. Groups of students can take over a discussion for a particular week and guide the discussion: asking questions, creating landscape posts, and even adding the wrap-up post. Or, if you're not comfortable turning over an entire discussion to the students, you can just assign the wrap-up post to a particular student each week. That way the students gain ownership in the course and also exercise their critical thinking skills. Our goal is always to not only create a good discussion but also give students the skills to lead their own discussions on interesting ideas.

Interview with Jed Duggan, IDEAL New Mexico

Teacher Jed Duggan started his career being antitechnology. He says he was very traditional and tied to a textbook. But then, during his first year of teaching, he taught next to an extremely innovative educator who used technology throughout his classes. When Duggan saw the results, he knew that technology was something he needed to explore more. Now, Duggan is an online teacher, a traditional face-to-face teacher, and a PhD student focused on the uses of technology in all three roles. He's seen the promise of this form of education and wants to find ways to do it better.

Duggan teaches economics and world geography for IDEAL New Mexico, a state-run virtual program with supplemental courses for students throughout the state. Discussion boards are an integral part of every unit in his courses. Duggan says they add an interactive element that would be sorely missed if they didn't exist. Without discussions, you could become isolated in your learning. Instead, using discussions provides additional perspectives beyond the teacher and a true, authentic audience for your ideas.

One of the things that Duggan has been working on in his online discussions is to help students understand how to disagree in a respectful way. It's a real balance. You want to promote netiquette with your students and also give them the freedom to challenge each other. A first step in that process is to help students get to know each other better. By hosting regular webinars, Duggan helps his students get comfortable with each other and prime the pump for later discussions. He also models appropriate disagreement by playing devil's advocate in the discussion boards. Through Duggan's posts that question the standard thinking, students can see that there are ways to disagree without being offensive.

Although Duggan really values discussion boards in his fully online class and in his traditional courses, he knows that they can be intimidating for some students. As a workaround, he'll occasionally let students e-mail him their response to the discussion board. Then, he'll post their response so that it stays anonymous. It's a way to get their voices heard but also provides some anonymity for them.

All in all, Duggan finds that discussions provide a powerful forum in the online course and should be a valued part of any online teacher's routine. His best piece of advice for online teachers is to find a way to reflect and wrap up a discussion when it's complete. Students need that closure. Posting a Wordle of the discussion (where the ideas that are mentioned the most appear in larger type) can be a great way to help students see the key ideas (www.wordle.net).

FOCUS ON BLENDED LEARNING

There are some really fantastic options for using discussion boards in a blended environment. In some ways, you can use the best of both worlds! Students can gain experience speaking in front of a crowd and also have the more private and sometimes anonymous experience of having a discussion in an online forum. One way to manage a hybrid discussion is to begin the discussion in the face-to-face portion of your class and then wrap it up in an online discussion. That way all the voices in the room get heard and you're not limited to a forty-five-minute class. You could also invert those options and open a discussion online while wrapping up with some of the most interesting ideas from the online portion in a face-to-face concluding discussion. The options are endless and they can be an exciting way to enrich your classroom! For more ideas on using discussions in a blended classroom, check out chapter 14.

CHAPTER SEVEN

TEACHING SYNCHRONOUS SESSIONS

ESSENTIAL QUESTIONS:

- What are the basic functionalities in a webinar tool?

- What function do synchronous sessions serve in an online classroom?

- How long should an effective synchronous session be?

- What kinds of activities should be included in a synchronous session?

- What should be done if a student can't attend a synchronous session?

Although facilitating a discussion board might be one of the most foreign things a new online teacher does, teaching a synchronous session or webinar will be one of the most familiar tasks for a teacher who is transitioning from a traditional face-to-face classroom. A synchronous session is basically a webinar in which all the students in your class are in a virtual space at the same time. The teacher is talking via a microphone and all of the students are listening at the

Note: The terms *synchronous session, webinar,* and *live session* are used interchangeably throughout this chapter. They all refer to when students and the teacher are coming together at the same time to share in a learning experience in a virtual space.

same time. Students are able to talk and use the chat functions to interact live. The teacher is able to present content via a whiteboard or PowerPoint and students are able to ask questions instantaneously. Although the tool is almost science fiction in its capabilities, you'll find that many of the tasks are quite familiar from your days in a traditional classroom.

Synchronous sessions serve a very important function in an online classroom. They can be a time to clarify directions and regroup your students. They allow students to hear your voice and get to know who you are. They can also be a great time for students to socialize and really get to know each other. All of these functions can happen in that online webinar space. However, there are also some huge pitfalls to avoid. You never want your webinar to be sit-and-get lectures. Your students will check out and start watching TV or surfing Facebook (and you'll never know the difference!). It's absolutely vital to make your online webinars as engaging as possible so that students want to be a part of them and they become a vital function of your classroom. In this chapter, we'll explore how to make that happen.

BASIC CAPABILITIES OF SYNCHRONOUS TOOLS

First, let's start by exploring the basic functions of a synchronous tool. There are several great synchronous tools on the market today. Blackboard Collaborate, WebEx, and Adobe Connect are just a few. The screenshot shown in figure 7.1 from Blackboard Collaborate is representative of the layout of most tools.

You can see that along the left-hand side students have access to a microphone tool to be able to talk to the rest of the class. They can also use the webcam and video tool to broadcast a live picture while talking. There are also tools to be able to virtually raise their hand or participate in a poll. The chat function allows them to interact at any time with the teacher or the rest of the class. In the middle of the screen is an interactive whiteboard where the teacher can present content or draw something to demonstrate a concept. There are also tools in that space for displaying a website or displaying a portion of your screen to the entire class. You'll also notice that there's a record button available so that any live session can be recorded and shared with students who are unable to be in the room during the actual session. All of these tools provide a huge variety of options within a synchronous session. Ideally, you'll use several of the tools within a live session to create a valuable learning experience for your students. Next, let's explore best practices for each of these tools.

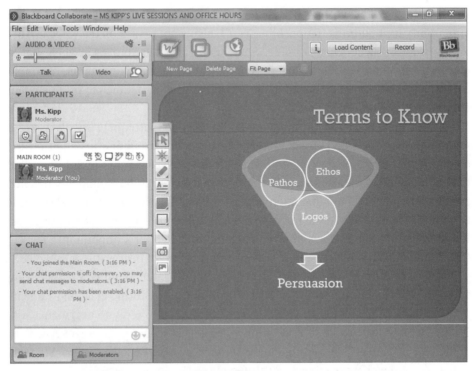

Figure 7.1   Blackboard Collaborate Synchronous Tool Example

COMMUNICATION TOOLS: MICROPHONE, VIDEO, CHAT, AND POLLING

Arguably the most important tools you'll have in your live sessions are the communication tools. These are the tools that allow you to interact with your students in the webinar in much the same way you might in a face-to-face meeting.

The microphone tool allows you to talk to the class. In order to use this tool well, it's important to have a high-quality headset to use when teaching live sessions. That way your sound is clearer and you're less likely to pick up a lot of background noise, feedback, or echo from your office while you're teaching. For most of the meeting, you'll wind up leaving your microphone on and interacting with the class in that way. I'd advise testing the microphone a few minutes before class to make sure that everyone can hear you. It gives students a chance to troubleshoot their speakers and make sure everything is working as it should. That troubleshooting time is also great for sharing personal stories with students and asking them about how things are going in their lives. Kids need to socialize with each other and with you and that time before a live session provides an opportunity for building relationships. You'll also want to turn on the webcam tool during webinars whenever possible. Students love to see your face when you're teaching them and it adds a very personal element to the live session. Yes, that means you'll have to get cleaned up before a live session but the payoff in student engagement is worth it!

You'll also occasionally want your students to participate in class via a microphone on their end. I ask students to have a microphone installed on the computer that they'll use to attend live sessions. Then, when it's really important to hear a lengthy response to a question or when I want to have students practice public speaking, we'll use that microphone tool in class. You will find that students are pretty reluctant to use the microphone and will come up with a lot of excuses. It's intimidating to broadcast your voice to the world and it's important to respect that. I only push the issue when it's absolutely vital that I hear a student's voice.

Instead of the microphone tool, students generally interact with the class during a live session via the chat function. I ask a lot of questions during class and students use the chat tool to reply. I generally ask every student to reply to every question. It takes time for everyone to type in their responses so it's good for everyone to participate instead of just waiting on one student to answer each question. Students will also use the chat area to ask clarifying questions for you as well.

The final communication tool that you'll find yourself using frequently is the polling tool. The polling tool allows you to ask questions of the class and collect responses on the fly. There are usually two different poll options. The first one is a yes-no option. I use this quite a bit to quickly assess understanding. I might say, ''Give me a green check mark if this assignment makes sense. Give me a red X if you still have questions.'' When I was in a face-to-face classroom, I had students give me a thumbs up or down. The yes-no polling feature gives me a similar tool but it also makes sure that students are still engaged with the class. If I ask a yes-no question and a student does not respond at all in the polling area, I know that he or she is not engaged with the class. I also use the yes-no polling feature for housekeeping items such as, ''Give me a green check mark if you're hearing me OK. I want to make sure my microphone is working!'' For more complex polling tasks, there's also a multiple choice polling option. When you turn this on for students, they can choose A, B, C, or D for a particular option. It can be a great way to give a pop quiz or quickly survey students about an issue. For example, I might say, ''Let's talk about where you'd like this semester's field trip to be. Hit 'A' if you'd like to go to the art museum, hit 'B' if you'd like to go to a Shakespearean play, hit 'C' if you'd like to go to the science museum, or hit 'D' if you have another idea.'' Student responses can then be anonymously shared with the class. The polling tools will quickly become a critical part of every live session because they are an invaluable way to keep students engaged with what you're discussing.

PRESENTATION TOOLS: WHITEBOARD, SCREEN SHARING, AND FILE SHARING

In addition to interacting with students via the communication tools, you'll also need to share content in your live session. The easiest space to share content is in the virtual whiteboard. On this whiteboard you'll have the option of typing information, highlighting, creating shapes, writing freehand, and so on. Just like in your face-to-face classroom, the whiteboard is a space to share content and demonstrate ideas. In its most basic form, you can simply write an agenda on the whiteboard and then demonstrate all your content for a session via that tool.

Although it can be effective to simply type or draw all your content during a session, you'll also have the option of uploading a PowerPoint to your interactive whiteboard. Sharing something that's more visually appealing can help draw your students into the session and make your content more clear. For me, it's also a great way to keep class moving. I design the class in PowerPoint and then use the PowerPoint during the live session to keep myself on track and efficient. Otherwise the session can lose its focus.

At first, you'll probably just use the whiteboard tool to share a PowerPoint or visual presentation. However, as your skills get more advanced you'll also want to start using that area to share your screen. Basically, the screen-share tool allows you to share a portion of your computer screen with the whole class. Then, instead of being confined to the content of a PowerPoint, you're able to use any application on your computer or on the web to demonstrate class content. I've regularly done a screen share to show students the course calendar, to walk them through course content, to demonstrate a tool they'll be using during the week, or to even open a Word document and create something together. The possibilities are endless and it can be a great way to share your ideas!

The next presentation tool that you may use is the web-sharing tool. Although the screen-sharing tool just shows students a portion of your screen, this tool allows you to navigate to a particular website on the interactive whiteboard and then give students the option to navigate through the site themselves. You can start out demonstrating the website to students but then, when they're ready, you can allow them to control the navigation for the whole class instead. It can be a great way to explore a site together and still allow the teacher to be the captain of the ship.

The final presentation tool that you may find yourself using on a regular basis is the file-sharing tool. This tool allows you to ''push'' a file to the entire class. Instead of opening the file on the screen, the system actually opens a dialogue box on all students' screens so they can download a file to their hard drives. I use this tool to make sure that all students have a copy of essential files for the upcoming week that may not be in the regular course content. For example, I might have additional examples for a project or a more in-depth rubric that I share during the live session. Students soon realize that not only are live sessions helpful for understanding content, they also make the work during the week much easier!

Although there are many other tools that are available in a webinar tool, these are the ones you'll find yourself using most often. They can be combined in hundreds of ways to make for a really interactive, engaging session for students.

TIME CONSIDERATIONS

Although live sessions are a critical component of an online course, how large a part they play in your instruction will vary greatly depending on your teaching model. Some programs ask teachers to provide a live session every day. Others ask for once a week. Others ask for optional tutoring sessions only. There is quite a bit of variety depending on student needs and program philosophy.

I think a word of caution is in order here about how we use synchronous sessions. It is possible to overuse synchronous sessions to the point that they become ineffective. The greatest strength of online learning is its flexibility. If we require students to be on a computer at a certain time of day every day for synchronous sessions, we have handicapped the model. It is no longer flexible and therefore is less effective for students. We want to use the strength of our online teaching tools to the best of our ability and a webinar is best used as a supplement to the learning, not as the core instructional tool.

In my teaching situation, I teach one live session per week per course. In that session I demonstrate the most difficult concept of the coming week. We also usually spend some time working on an assignment from the upcoming week together when I'm there as a mentor and guide for that work. The bulk of my instruction happens asynchronously outside of the webinar and I prefer it that way. I want to use the incredible tools of the online classroom to create really strong learning experiences for students. The webinar tool is there to supplement that instruction but it is only a supplement. The real learning happens in the online course content.

There is some debate about how long a synchronous session should last. In general students will lose interest after about twenty minutes of a webinar. If that webinar is extremely interactive, you might be able to hold their attention for forty minutes. However, any longer than that and you will have students multitasking during your class session. They'll be watching TV, surfing the Internet, or working on another class and that's the last thing you want. I aim for a thirty-minute session each time, with the entire session packed with interactive activities and no more than ten minutes of teacher talk. The focus should be on active learning, even when the tool is a webinar.

You'll also want to think critically about the needs of your students when you schedule your live sessions. Early mornings are generally bad times for teenagers. They're not awake yet and thus are unable to interact with you on a deep level. Because you don't have to start your bell schedule at 7 A.M., it's best not to! For flexibility's sake, I generally host my live sessions in the late afternoon, around four o'clock. That way students who have jobs or attend other schools part-time can generally find a way to attend. If at all possible, poll your students to see what works for their schedule and then set up your sessions accordingly. You won't be able to get all the students there live but you want as many as possible.

MAKING UP MISSED SESSIONS

Unfortunately not all of your students will be able to attend your live sessions at the scheduled time. Many, if not the majority, will have to watch a recording at a later time. Although that's unfortunate, it's a reality that you'll need to plan for. There are a few ways to approach the problem.

The first way to manage the problem is to make live sessions an optional part of your course. Then students can watch the live sessions as they need to in order to access content. If you choose this option, be aware that your attendance may drop in live sessions. That's OK. Students who need the help will use it. Those who don't will be able to use their time more efficiently in working on their assignments. You may have to realize that not all students will need to hear your voice in order to complete course content. That's humbling but perhaps a reality. If you choose this option, you'll also find yourself referring students to the recordings quite a bit. Until they realize how helpful those sessions are, they may choose not to watch them. Then, when they are stuck on a concept, they'll e-mail you for help. Your job will be to refer them to the recording for a detailed explanation, letting them know to e-mail again if they still don't understand after watching the recording. It's a frustrating side effect but, again, all part of the process.

The other way to handle students who don't attend live sessions is to create a makeup assignment for each session. Basically, students who attend the class live get full credit for a live session with no additional work. Then, those who can't attend are required to watch the recorded session and complete a related assignment in order to earn their points. Sometimes that assignment is to write a summary of the session. Other times that assignment may be to complete the same tasks that we did during the session. It can vary. This option has the benefit of making sure every student watches the live session. However, it can also feel like jumping through hoops for students. I've had students who have told me that watching the recording is a waste of time because they can complete all the assignments without the live sessions. Is it fair to make all students watch a recording if not all students need to? That will be a personal decision based on your teaching philosophy.

Personally, I've experimented with both of these options for dealing with nonattenders to live sessions. I was not fully happy with either and I'm still searching for an option that is fair to students but also values our time in live sessions. I'll continue to experiment but there may be no perfect solution.

BUILDING A ROUTINE

In addition to meeting at a regular time that is accessible to all students, you'll want to explore creating a regular routine for each live session. Just as in a face-to-face classroom, students like to know what to expect when they get together. Currently, this is the routine that each of my live sessions follows:

- Welcome time (approximately two minutes): I usually share a personal, funny story with students. I ask them how things are going in class and touch base on their lives.

- Announcements (approximately five minutes): I verbally explain some of the most important announcements for class. This usually includes due date reminders, items for the larger school, and information about upcoming units. I also take questions about these items.

- Preview (no more than five minutes): I preview the work of the upcoming week. I might share my screen and walk through the assignments or I may just verbally explain them. I want students to have a clear understanding of the objectives we're trying to meet in that week's work in addition to understanding which assignments are due when. In weeks when students are using a particularly difficult tool, I may also demonstrate that tool during this time.

- Lecture (no more than five minutes): I use this time to verbally explain some of the most difficult concepts in the week's work.

- Demonstration or discussion (approximately ten minutes): This is the most valuable part of the class. This is where we work together on an assignment from the upcoming week. I will open a Word document and screen share or turn on the whiteboard tools and work together. Alternatively, we may have a live discussion or an interesting idea from the week's work (either the previous week or the upcoming week).

- Question and answer (as much time as needed): Finally, I'll open up the class for questions. Students can ask about their grades, clarify concepts, or whatever else they may need. When they feel their questions are fully answered, they're free to exit the webinar.

I find this routine to be extremely helpful for students. They know what to expect and the webinar keeps moving at a good pace. You'll need to find a routine that works for you and for your students.

ACTIVITY IDEAS

As you begin to plan for your first synchronous sessions, you may find that the biggest challenge is planning for that demonstration section of the class. Because you are not meeting face-to-face, it can be a challenge to come up with ways to have students interact on a meaningful level within the webinar tool. Following are just a few examples of activities that work well during the demonstration time and that can be adapted for any subject area:

- *Scavenger hunt:* In this activity, give students a topic that you want them to research. For example, you might tell students that you want them to find out as much as they can about Stalin's early childhood. Then, give them five to ten minutes to open a new window and complete their research. During that time, turn off the microphone and let them work. At the end of that time, each student shares his or her findings with the class via the chat box, microphone, or whiteboard. You can then highlight the most important findings and relate them to the content of the upcoming week.

- *Shared authoring:* In this activity, you open a word processing document on your computer and do a screen share so that all students have access to the chat box and can also see the word processing document. Then, working together, the class creates a sample response to one of the questions or assignments in that week's work. Each student contributes a portion of the work and you demonstrate how to pull all the content together into an exemplary assignment.

- *Shared reading:* Put a portion of subject-related text on the whiteboard screen in the webinar tool. Then give students access to all the whiteboard tools and ask them to highlight the most important portions of the text. Once all the students have highlighted a portion, each student shares why he or she thinks that's important information from the text and you explain how that portion of text relates to the content in the week's work.

- *Visual thinking:* After explaining a difficult concept from the week's work, bring up a blank whiteboard and turn on all the whiteboard tools for students. Students then take turns illustrating the concept they just discussed by drawing various elements of the system. If permitted, they can also copy and paste images onto the whiteboard that help them to remember the concepts. By the end, the class has created a powerful mnemonic for the content.

In this whirlwind of a chapter we have just touched on the basics of how to create a successful synchronous session. The real key is to make sure that no live session feels like sit and get. Students should be actively engaged with the content and their teacher, just as they should be in a face-to-face classroom. The only real difference is the venue. With practice, you'll find that teaching webinars each week is an important part of your job and, I hope, an enjoyable one.

FOCUS ON BLENDED LEARNING

Because a blended classroom incorporates some face-to-face time, teachers probably will not have a reason to teach many synchronous sessions or webinars as a part of the core curriculum of the class. The function of the synchronous session can instead be fulfilled through a face-to-face teaching session. However, there are still several ways to use synchronous sessions as a supplement to a blended classroom that will make the course more successful and more engaging.

One way is that synchronous sessions can be provided for office hours or study times during the online portion of a course. Students can stop by a synchronous webinar to get help from the teacher or help each other with assignments that are happening in the asynchronous or online environment. That real time help can prevent students from feeling isolated and help to deepen a classroom community.

Another way a webinar tool can be used in a blended course is for making easy, quick tutorial videos. Even without an audience, a teacher can record a quick lecture or tutorial on an important concept inside a webinar tool and then embed that recording throughout the online portion of the course. Oftentimes students appreciate the ability to hear content again, pause, and even rewind to crucial points of instruction. For some students, that extra instruction will mean the difference between moving smoothly through the course or having to contact the teacher for additional help. As an added bonus, these quick tutorials could even be recorded during a face-to-face class meeting. A basic audio or video recorder can record what was shared in class and then preserve it as a future reference.

One other way to use a webinar tool in a blended course is to provide just-in-time help for students who are struggling with content or with technical problems in the online portion of the course. Lots of problems can be quickly resolved by meeting in a webinar tool and doing a quick screen share. By seeing the screen the student is working on, the teacher can help resolve any technical issues and see exactly where the breakdown in understanding is happening. It might take upwards of ten e-mails to discover a problem that could be easily solved in a simple three-minute synchronous session. Those sessions can be huge time-savers.

Synchronous webinars and recording tools are important tools in a blended teacher's arsenal, whether for tutoring, video recording, or working one-on-one with students, and it's important not to overlook them.

CHAPTER EIGHT

CREATING AND MODIFYING ASSIGNMENTS

ESSENTIAL QUESTIONS:

- What are the qualities of a good assignment in an online classroom?

- How can an online teacher create un-Googleable assignments?

- In what ways can the online learning platform create experiences that aren't possible face-to-face?

It's every online teacher's worst nightmare. You're hired to teach a new online course in the fall. The course is already created, it's on an interesting topic, and you're thrilled to begin. Then, when August rolls around and you get course access, you open the course only to find that it's wholly inadequate for teaching the content. Instead of a robust course that includes critical thinking and in-depth interaction with content, it's a point-and-click course with almost no critical thinking and no collaboration. Students may gain information about the content but they won't have a robust learning experience. Instead they'll stare at a screen and click on multiple-choice icons. This is obviously unacceptable but the question becomes, "What can you do?" In this chapter we'll explore what makes a good assignment in an online classroom and brainstorm some ways to create and modify assignments for your online courses.

DEFINING A GOOD ASSIGNMENT

Great assignments in an online course can come in all forms. Wikis, blogs, worksheets, and even quizzes all have their place. The real key is to ensure that every assignment you have students complete is of the highest quality possible and engages their mind in addition to their clicker finger!

iNACOL has identified several key elements of quality assignments in their National Standards for Quality Online Courses. (You can see the complete list of iNACOL course standards in appendix A.) Here are a few that can help you to evaluate a particular assignment and see if it should be left alone, modified, or cut from your course:

- *Standard A2:* The course content and assignments are aligned with the state's content *standards*, common core curriculum, or other accepted content standards set for Advanced Placement courses, technology, computer science, or other courses whose content is not included in the state standards.

- *Standard A3:* The course content and assignments are of sufficient *rigor, depth, and breadth* to teach the standards being addressed.

- *Standard B3:* The course instruction includes activities that engage students in *active learning*.

- *Standard B4:* The course and course instructor provide students with *multiple learning paths*, based on student needs, that engage students in a variety of ways.

- *Standard B5:* The course provides opportunities for students to engage in *higher-order thinking*, critical reasoning activities, and thinking in increasingly complex ways.

- *Standard D4: Rich media* are provided in multiple formats for ease of use and access in order to address diverse student needs.

For each assignment that you have doubts about, it can be helpful to look through it using the indicators in italics. If an assignment meets the qualifications, it can be fine to leave it in your course without modifications. However, if it doesn't, further work should be done to improve the quality of the assignment. Let's take a look at an example assignment.

Assignment for a math course: Please solve for *x* in each of the following equations and submit to the Dropbox.

1. $4x + 3 = 27$
2. $(6 + x)3 = 45$
3. $82 - x = 63 + 12$

Although this assignment would technically demonstrate that a student understands how to solve for an unknown in an equation (a basic math standard), it doesn't meet some of the core qualifications of a good assignment in an online course. First, students are not actively demonstrating their knowledge of the subject. They're not creating anything new with the content or demonstrating that they truly understand what it means for an equation to contain an unknown. Instead, they are demonstrating basic problem solving. Second, the assignment doesn't allow students to demonstrate their knowledge through multiple learning paths. They must plug and chug in text, with no other way to demonstrate knowledge. Finally, the assignment is lacking in rich media that could make it far more engaging and demonstrate more lasting knowledge.

Consider if the assignment instead read this way:

1. Solve for *x* in the following equation and explain in a paragraph how you found your answer: $4x + 3 = 27$.

2. Create a real-world scenario in which this equation would apply: $(6 + x)3 = 45$.

3. Pretend you are a math tutor for a student living in Indonesia. She is struggling with the concept of how to solve for an unknown and needs you to demonstrate. Please make a video, using the tool of your choice, to show her how to solve for an unknown in this equation: $82 - x = 63 + 12$. Some tools you might consider are a basic video recorder (on a phone or otherwise), a Jing screencast, or an Audacity audio recording.

In question one, the simple addition of a writing portion will help students better demonstrate understanding and make the problem harder to plug into an online calculator. In question two, students have to demonstrate that they not only understand how to solve for an unknown but that they also understand what kinds of real-world situations would involve unknowns. Finally, in question three, students need to use rich media to demonstrate their understanding of the process in a very tangible way for their instructor.

You can see that instruction like this may require more time for the student and the teacher. Meaningful questions require time and care to construct and to answer but the result is deeper learning for students and much more engaging assignments.

Although the iNACOL standards provide an excellent framework for evaluating an assignment, I believe that any given assignment can be evaluated even more simply by asking four key questions:

- Does the assignment align with standards?

- Is the assignment engaging?

- Does the assignment require critical thinking?

- Can the assignment be easily looked up on Google?

If the answer to any one of those questions is no, then the teacher has an ethical obligation to revise the assignment to better meet student needs. For some assignments, that revision might be fairly minor. For other assignments, it will require a complete overhaul. However, it is absolutely worth it in order to provide a quality learning experience for every student, in every assignment.

CREATING UN-GOOGLEABLE ASSIGNMENTS

The last key question deserves a little more attention. One of the concerns that opponents of online learning constantly bring up is that the learning is not valid because it is too easy to cheat. This is a valid worry. More and more, some of the core assignments for major online course providers are showing up in Yahoo! Answers and WikiAnswers. This kind of cheating is particularly prevalent because it is so easy to do. Students simply need to type a quiz question into Google and five seconds later they have the answer. As long as they then put that answer into their own words, there's no way a teacher can even know that they've cheated. It's invisible cheating and allowing it to happen in our online courses is professionally irresponsible. It becomes our ethical duty to modify assignments so that they are no longer Googleable and student learning is more valid.

So then, what does an un-Googleable assignment look like? Because the Internet is growing each year and getting more and more sophisticated, is it even possible to create something that can't be looked up? The answer is yes. The real key lies in asking interesting questions that value application more than knowledge on Bloom's taxonomy. The lower levels of Bloom's are easily looked up using an Internet search engine or Wikipedia. Higher-level thinking skills, however, are much more difficult to find. As an added bonus, they're also the kinds of thinking we want students to be doing anyway.

One of my favorite un-Googleable assignments asks students to create a fictional conversation between two characters in stories that we've been reading. For example, they might create a situation in which Daisy from *The Great Gatsby* runs into Juliet from *Romeo and Juliet*. The student then creates a pretend conversation between the two characters and writes up the transcript of their chat. What might they find to talk about? What do they have in common? How do their two stories run parallel? The assignment requires that students have read the two stories but it also challenges them to compare and contrast at a deep level, in addition to engaging in creative writing.

A colleague of mine has students create a class newspaper as a final project in a US history course. The teacher provides the students with a date for the newspaper and then students are required to research what events were happening on that day as well as review the national climate during that time period. They then take those events and write up a series of newspaper articles for that day's headlines. It's a fascinating project that requires students to complete in-depth research via an Internet search engine and then transform that research into something completely different, something not easily found and not easily plagiarized. The learning is deep and also requires a whole range of valuable skills: writing, researching, summarizing, and evaluating. Assignments like these should make up at least 70 percent of any given online course so that we can ensure that students are not just regurgitating information but are also processing it at deep levels.

At a conference I recently attended, an attendee challenged me on the idea of the un-Googleable assignment. He said that we want to make sure students know how to use the Internet wisely, not that we don't want them to use it. I absolutely agree! To clarify, in the ideal un-Googleable assignment, students would still use Google (or another search engine) to find their basic information. However, that's not where the assignment ends. To be a valuable learning experience, students need to then transform what they found in a search engine into something completely new. In doing so, they've demonstrated deep understanding rather than just the ability to cut and paste.

KEEPING YOUR COURSE CURRENT

This issue of creating un-Googleable assignments is one that is particularly sticky because we're aiming at a moving target. Unfortunately, if an assignment is not revised for several years in a course, the assignment very quickly becomes Googleable because students post the question and their ideas to various social media. Every few years a course is taught, the assignments need to be updated accordingly so that they remain valuable, in-depth learning experiences.

USING THE PLATFORM TO CREATE UNIQUE EXPERIENCES

One of the other points you'll want to consider in creating assignments for your online classroom is that the online platform allows you to create experiences that aren't possible anywhere else. From collaborative wikis to digital storytelling to in-depth discussions, there are some activities that can *only* happen in the online classroom or happen much more effectively in that space. You'll want to take a critical look at the assignments in your course and make sure you're using all the tools of the online classroom to your advantage. Your students deserve the very best.

Interview with Jeff Simmons, Idaho Digital Learning Academy

Jeff Simmons has been teaching online since 2001. Since then, he's moved through many different roles from course developer to online teacher to trainer, and now to instructional manager overseeing the online teachers in his school, Idaho Digital Learning Academy (IDLA). IDLA is a state-supported supplemental online program.

Simmons says that the biggest change when he moved into online teaching was the flexibility. Kids had flexible time to complete their assignments and his work became very flexible as well. Because IDLA takes students from across the state, Simmons also began teaching a much more diverse population.

Simmons says that one of his best pieces of advice for new online teachers is to be reflective. At the end of any given semester, you should take an honest look at what you do well and what you could improve on. Then take the things you could improve on and pick one to focus on for the next semester. Simmons says it's amazing how much progress you can make over time! This is especially true with creating course content because once you improve the content that new content will carry on to the next several groups of students you teach.

FOCUS ON BLENDED LEARNING

The blended learning environment provides the unique opportunity to create assignments that bridge the digital divide, incorporating face-to-face and online elements, truly the best of both worlds. An assignment might begin with a face-to-face discussion and brainstorming session and then move into the creation of an online wiki as students are completing their research. Then that wiki could morph into a final presentation shared in front of a real audience in the classroom. The possibilities are extremely powerful. For some examples of assignments that do just this, check out chapter 14.

CHAPTER NINE

COLLABORATING IN ONLINE COURSES

ESSENTIAL QUESTIONS:

- What kinds of assignments can be created for students to be able to connect with each other?

- What are basic course tools that encourage student collaboration?

WHY COLLABORATION IS ESSENTIAL

As discussed in chapter 2, it's absolutely essential to the success of an online course that students are not working in isolation. They should feel connected with you as the teacher but also connected with each other. That can happen in several ways. One is through discussion boards. The other is through shared experiences in the course. Those shared experiences are assignments in which students are working together to create a shared product. In this chapter we'll explore how to create assignments in which students are collaborating to create shared products that deepen their learning.

WIKIS

One of the easiest ways to have students collaborate in a course is via a wiki. The word *wiki* is Hawaiian for *easy*. A wiki is just a website that's very easy for multiple people to edit. It is a powerful tool that can be used throughout your course.

Wikispaces and Google Sites are probably the easiest tools to use to set up a wiki for your students. For those using Blackboard as your LMS, there's also a wiki tool built right in to the course system. Your first step in creating a wiki assignment is to build the wiki itself. It works best if you create a structure for the wiki first and then ask students to flesh out the details. For example, I use a wiki assignment in a unit on *Hamlet*. I tell students that their goal is to create a study guide for *Hamlet*, much like the ones you might find on SparkNotes. I create pages in the wiki for character summaries, act summaries, study questions, symbols, and so on. Then I ask students to contribute to the wiki in at least three places each and flesh out all the details. The screenshot in Figure 9.1 shows what the wiki looks like when students begin.

When the students finish adding to the wiki, they have a really in-depth resource to refer to throughout the unit. In addition, there's a sense of accomplishment and camaraderie in knowing that they worked together to create a really amazing final product.

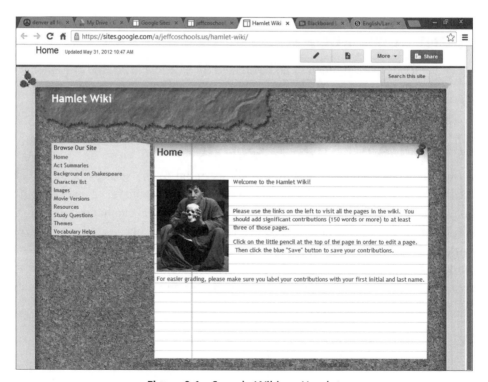

Figure 9.1 Sample Wiki on *Hamlet*

Wikis can be used in lots of different ways in your course. If students are researching various topics in your content area, they can contribute the information they're finding to a class wiki. If students are reviewing for a final exam, they can work together to create a wiki with all the pertinent content. It's a really powerful tool for creating collaborative learning experiences.

BLOGS

Another tool you'll want to consider using with your students is a blog. Traditionally, blogs are used for individuals to process their ideas on a topic and share them with the world. However, they can also be used for an entire group to blog together and create a shared final product. Blogging tools such as WordPress and Blogger can make the process easy. Many LMSs even include a blogging tool right in the LMS interface to allow easy integration of a blog into your course.

I recently used a blog with an undergraduate educational technology course. I set up one blog in Blogger and then added all the students as blog authors. Then, students were responsible for adding blog posts throughout the semester processing what they were learning in class. The final product was a fascinating collection of their evolving ideas on what's possible in educational technology. Topics varied from ''Using texting in the classroom'' to ''Using (not resisting) technology.'' Because we shared the journal entries in a blog format rather than in a traditional Dropbox, students immediately had an authentic audience—each other as well as the world.

Blogs work well any time you want students to process what they're learning in writing and share it collaboratively. Blogs can be used initially in a unit to access background information, they can be used in the middle of a unit as a learning log, or they can be used at the end of a unit as a culminating activity. Perhaps the most powerful way to use a blog is to introduce it at the beginning of a unit and have students add to it throughout the course of their learning. By the end, the blog is an in-depth artifact of the learning that's happened.

GOOGLE DOCS

The Google Docs suite of tools also provides an interesting way for students to collaborate. Google Docs provides word processor, spreadsheet, presentation, and drawing tools for free online (https://docs.google.com). Within each one of those tools, there is a share option for students to share a file with another student in real time. They can then each work on the document together, creating a shared project in the tool. Once an assignment is complete, they just share it and add the teacher to the file for grading. The possibilities are endless and extremely powerful for learning!

I recently had an encounter with a student in Google Docs that demonstrated the immense power of the tool. The student was writing a graduation speech. She had trouble sharing the file with me so we decided to share it via Google Docs instead. Then we met together in Google Docs at a designated time to work on revisions. We were able to use the chat feature to go through the paper line by line and revise. Then, when the student was making changes in the text itself, I could watch the process happening and redirect as needed. When needed, I was able to type in the text also and show the student different ways to correct the errors. It was a powerful learning experience for both of us. I could imagine using the tool for students to work with each other on revisions and create new products together.

The Google Drawing tools within Google Docs also have a lot of potential for students creating products together. The tools allow visual learners to represent their thinking in a new way. Figure 9.2 is a Google drawing created by two students to demonstrate their understanding of *Fahrenheit 451*.

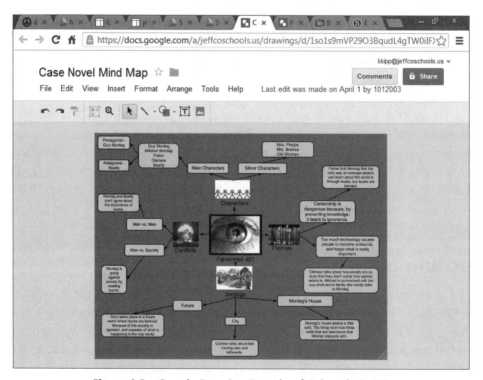

Figure 9.2   Google Drawing Sample of *Fahrenheit 451*

The project served two purposes. One, the students showed me that they were reading the text and understood it. Two, they worked together to compromise on how to word their ideas and represent them visually. That's powerful collaboration that can only happen when using a digital tool effectively.

E-PORTFOLIOS

Another possibility for student collaboration is through the use of e-portfolios. An e-portfolio is basically a collection of a student's work over the course of a semester. The students share how they have grown during the course and where they hope to grow in the future. Those portfolios are then shared with the rest of the class and students provide feedback to each other. The project has an authentic audience and is a powerful way to showcase learning.

For example, in an introduction to composition course, students shared the essays they had written all semester in a final web portfolio. Students loved seeing each other's work and felt a sense of accomplishment in putting together their portfolio that showcased their progress. It was also a great artifact to share with their parents. The students also gained experience in creating a website using Weebly, an easy website creation tool (www.weebly.com). Another tool that students can use is Google Sites, which has basic templates available for creating a website and sharing content. If you'd rather students didn't have to make a website in order to share their portfolio content, another option to consider is Pathbrite (www.pathbrite.com). Pathbrite is specifically a portfolio tool that allows students to add files of various types and then share them with one link. The graphic interface is beautiful and professional for a really amazing portfolio in a short period of time.

COLLABORATIVE GROUPS

In these examples, students were coming together to collaborate on a particular assignment. However, you'll also want to explore designs in which students are not necessarily creating anything together but are instead using each other as a resource or source of discussion ideas.

Editing and Writing Groups

Editing and writing groups can work really well in an online classroom, especially with a consistent group throughout a semester. The same group of students can work together via Google Docs, a synchronous session, a discussion board, or e-mail to edit and revise each other's work any time there's a written assignment.

The students gain the benefit of having multiple editors but they also get to see lots of examples of a particular assignment done well, helping them to improve the quality of their work.

Reading Groups

Reading groups can also be really powerful in an online classroom. Students might work together for a period of four to six weeks to read a particular text and discuss it. Through in-depth discussions with a consistent small group, student's understanding of the text is stretched and deepened. It's amazing how deep a discussion can go when it's given the time to develop!

Jigsaw Groups

A jigsaw group can also be a great way to share new content. Similar to a traditional classroom, a jigsaw group meets first in ''expert'' groups to become experts on a particular topic. Then, the expert groups meet as jigsaw groups with one member from each of the expert groups. Each expert educates his or her group about the topic. By the end, all of the students have a basic understanding of the content covered by all the expert groups. This kind of activity can be done via a discussion board or within a synchronous session to help students collaboratively build knowledge.

Discussion Groups

The final type of group you'll want to explore is a discussion group. Sometimes an online class might have up to 150 students within one section of the course. That can be overwhelming when you have a discussion in class. If every student posts twice, there might be three hundred posts in a particular discussion. Instead, it can be helpful to create discussion groups. For each discussion topic, the students are responsible for discussing with a group of 20 students instead of 150. That way posts are more manageable and discussions can be deeper. You can leave students in static discussion groups all semester or you can choose to mix up the groups at different times. Either way, you're focusing a discussion by limiting its participants.

STAYING INVOLVED

Although all of these strategies are extremely effective for building student learning through collaboration, it's still vital that you as the teacher remain involved throughout. Group work always involves some challenges, both face-to-face and online. It'll be important for you to stay involved in each project to ensure that student learning is maximized. One way to do that is to make sure that your presence is felt in each group project. A periodic post on a group's discussion board will remind students that you're watching all the group's interactions and you're there to help. You can also regularly e-mail group members to see how things are going and offer your expert assistance. Proactive communication can help your groups function more smoothly throughout.

FOCUS ON BLENDED LEARNING

One of the biggest challenges of collaborative learning in an online space is getting all students up to speed on using the tools. Wikis, Google Docs, blogs, and so on all require some basic training in order to use them. Although that can be done with a Jing video or other tutorial, in a blended environment, you have the luxury of sharing the tools with students while they are in your face-to-face classroom. With any collaborative online project, it's wise to take a few moments at the beginning of the project and simply demonstrate the tools to your students. You can also have them start working on the project and the tool while everyone is in the same room at the same time. That way most of the troubleshooting happens in the classroom and students can get right to work once they're working on their own in the online environment!

CHAPTER TEN

DIFFERENTIATING ASSIGNMENTS

ESSENTIAL QUESTIONS:

- What is differentiation?

- How is differentiation different in an online environment than in a face-to-face classroom?

- What are some practical ways to differentiate content?

WHAT IS DIFFERENTIATION?

One of the major buzz words in education since the new millennium has been *differentiation*. At its core, the word just means *different*. Teachers who differentiate well are creating different learning paths for different students. For example, a student who really doesn't understand commas might spend time on just comma rules during a unit on grammar and another student who already fully understands commas would get to work on the use of semicolons instead, a skill she doesn't yet understand. These different learning paths create a much richer learning experience for all students and, in the end, create higher achievement for all.

There are a few different ways that you can think about differentiation. One way is to differentiate for a student's interest. If a particular student is really fascinated by golf, a differentiated assignment might allow him to indulge in that passion and also learn an important concept about geometry, for example. If a particular student can't get enough of world history but hates science, a differentiated assignment might ask her to research the historical development of a scientific concept, which encourages the student to understand the science but also rewards her with the historical research that she's so passionate about.

Another way to think about differentiation is to think about differentiating for skill levels. As already mentioned, if students are weak in a particular concept but strong in another, there's no reason to make them continually review the idea that they already fully understand. Instead, a differentiated assignment will have them focus on the areas in which they are personally weak. In a conversation with Karen Cator, director of the Office of Education Technology at the US Department of Education, she suggested that someday online learning systems might have a built-in "learning positioning system," like GPS, in which every student is regularly assessed and then course work is designed based on student weaknesses (Cator, personal conversation). This is a fascinating idea and shows some real potential for our online learning systems. Until that day, however, we can approximate that experience by creating learning environments in which students can complete varying tasks depending on their current skills.

Another way to think about differentiation is to think about differentiating the presentation of content for learning styles or multiple intelligences. All students are getting the same content but its presentation may vary depending on their needs. For students who are audiovisual learners, course content might be customized with a lot of videos and podcasts to enrich the ideas. For students who understand ideas best through mind mapping or conceptual representations of ideas, the course might be customized with a lot of interactive graphics to help them process the content. The way they learn the material is different depending on their needs.

A final way to think about differentiation is that students are all receiving the same content but they demonstrate their understanding of it in different ways. Students who are gifted in music may be given the option to write a song about a topic and record it for the class. Any given assignment may have four or five different options for ways to present the content, allowing students to have choice and learn through their strengths. Figure 10.1 shows the different ways we can think about differentiation for student learning.

The real bonus of differentiation in an online environment is that the issue of classroom management fades in the background. In a traditional classroom, differentiation is very difficult because it's hard to imagine what the rest of the class might be doing while you're working with a small group of students on a concept that they're struggling with. Online learning simply doesn't have that limitation. All students can be working on their own customized path depending

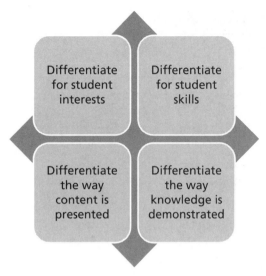

Figure 10.1 Ways to Differentiate Student Learning

on their needs. Not only do you not have to worry about what the rest of the class is doing, they are not worried about why one student gets something different. No one realizes the differences and thus everyone gets what they need.

Although differentiation has a lot of promise in the online classroom, the idea of designing a course for different learning paths can be overwhelming. In the rest of this chapter, we'll explore a few ways to differentiate that will not increase the teacher workload significantly.

CREATING CHOICE WITHIN ASSIGNMENTS

One of the easiest ways to differentiate within a course is to create student choice within an assignment. At the assignment level, you don't have to worry about creating different sessions for different students. Instead, every student receives the same directions and then has some choices about how to complete the assignment.

Just as there are different ways to differentiate, there are a couple of different ways to provide student choice in an assignment. The first way is to provide student choice in the content they'll be studying. It might be that all students need to study the Civil War but they can study various aspects of it. Some students might study medical care during the Civil War but others might focus on specific battles. All students are gaining knowledge about the topic but they have some choice in which specific subject they study. Then, later, they can come back together to share some of the things they learned with their classmates.

Exhibit 10.1. Vocabulary Magic

abate	conditional	haughty	provocative
abdicate	conformist	hedonist	prudent
aberration	convergence	hypothesis	querulous
abhor	deleterious	impetuous	rancorous
abstain	demagogue	impute	reclusive
adversity	digression	inconsequential	reconciliation
aesthetic	diligent	inevitable	renovation
amicable	discredit	intrepid	restrained
anachronistic	disdain	intuitive	reverence
arid	divergent	jubilation	sagacity
asylum	empathy	lobbyist	scrutinize
benevolent	emulate	longevity	spontaneous
bias	enervating	mundane	spurious
boisterous	ephemeral	nonchalant	submissive
brazen	evanescent	opulent	substantiate
brusque	exemplary	orator	subtle
camaraderie	extenuating	ostentatious	superficial
canny	florid	parched	superfluous
capacious	forbearance	perfidious	surreptitious
capitulate	fortitude	pragmatic	tactful
clairvoyant	fortuitous	precocious	tenacious
collaborate	foster	pretentious	transient
compassion	fraught	procrastinate	venerable
compromise	frugal	prosaic	vindicate
condescending	hackneyed	prosperity	wary

In one of my courses, I have a vocabulary assignment in which students get to choose twenty-five SAT words to focus on during the unit. Students choose terms they don't know and then they all complete the same assignments but use different words. Exhibit 10.1 shows what students would see when they begin the unit.

Did you know that the average person's vocabulary is about ten to fifteen thousand words? However, a highly educated person knows up to forty thousand words! That's a huge difference. Clearly, vocabulary is the door to higher education and higher comprehension.

In this unit you'll be choosing twenty-five words from a list of one hundred common SAT vocabulary words. Then, you'll be interacting deeply with those twenty-five words for the next two weeks. Although learning twenty-five new words may not change your entire vocabulary, it's a good start and along the way you'll practice lots of new ways to learn vocabulary.

The first step is to pick the twenty-five words you'd like to live with. Copy and paste the list into a word processing document. Then edit the list down until you have twenty-five words that you'd like to learn. **Choose words you do not yet know so that the exercises in this unit will be more meaningful!**

Students are really engaged during this unit because they get to choose the words they study. Occasionally a student will complain that he or she already knows all the words! In that case, we work together to create a customized list just for that student. I want everyone's needs to be met whenever possible.

The second way to differentiate within an assignment is to provide choice in the way that students demonstrate their knowledge on a particular topic. For example, at the end of the vocabulary unit shown in exhibit 10.1, students demonstrate their understanding of their new vocabulary words by participating in a ''getting creative'' assignment. In that assignment, they're given four different assignment options and must choose the one that sounds the most intriguing to them. All students are forced to be a bit creative but they can do it in different ways depending on their strengths. You can see the directions for that assignment in exhibit 10.2.

Exhibit 10.2. Getting Creative

Your next step will be to continue learning your words by creating something with them.

Choose *one* of these assignment options:

Art: Create vocabulary cartoons for at least ten of your twenty-five words. A vocabulary cartoon is a picture you draw (no copying and pasting!) that will help you remember your words. See examples here [put a link in here to different examples]. Because your cartoons must be hand drawn, you will need to take a picture of them or scan them in order to turn them in.

Music: For the musically inclined, write a song that includes at least fifteen of your words in the lyrics. Then use the microphone on your computer to record the song and submit your recording. Audacity (http://audacity.sourceforge .net) is a free program you can download for making recordings.

Games: Visit Discovery Education's Puzzlemaker (http://puzzlemaker.discoveryeducation.com/ CrissCrossSetupForm.asp). Make a word search and a crisscross puzzle using all twenty-five of your words. Print the puzzles and then solve them by hand. Finally, scan the puzzles or take a picture of them to submit.

Poetry: Create a twenty-line poem that includes at least fifteen of your vocabulary words. Rhyming is optional. Be sure you use all your words correctly!

Submit the assignment you chose.

Through this assignment, I'm able to see that all students understand their vocabulary words but they're demonstrating that knowledge in a variety of ways depending on their own strengths and interests.

CUSTOMIZED PATH THROUGH A SESSION OR UNIT

Another more complicated way to differentiate within an online course is to provide a customized path through a particular session. Early in a session, the course might ask students to choose a path or a path might be chosen based on their performance on a preassessment. Then all the assignments in that session would be customized based on the student's needs.

In my English 12 course, I have a differentiated session built for the beginning of my *Hamlet* unit. Some students have read Shakespeare before and feel confident tackling his work. Others have never read Shakespeare or have read it unsuccessfully in other classes. They need two very different introductions to Shakespeare's work. Therefore, the first session of the unit has them move into two groups. The students who are already confident tackling Shakespeare will focus on more complex ideas of theme and tragedy. Others who may struggle with the bard will focus on basic ideas of comprehension and language. Then, once they're ready, the two groups can come together again in the second session of the unit. They've both gotten what they needed in order to be successful with the rest of the play. To simplify recordkeeping, both groups submit the assignments from that session to the same Dropbox so I can easily grade them. Figure 10.2 shows what the session looks like on a student's screen.

The amazing thing is that students love this format. The students in group A really appreciate that they've gotten the support they needed in order to be successful. The students in group B appreciate that they've been challenged at an appropriate level. Once we finish this session, students consistently ask for more differentiated work. They love feeling like their needs have been met!

Once you've attempted to create a differentiated session, you can take the even bigger step of a differentiated unit. Students could move into two or three different units depending on their needs. They might share the same due dates over the course of a month but the entire unit is built to meet their interests, learning styles, or abilities. You can only imagine how engaging the course would be, even if that level of differentiation is attempted only once or twice during the course of the work!

CRITICAL PATHS

Up until now we've been focused on how differentiation can effectively challenge students based on their interests, learning styles, or skills. However, differentiation

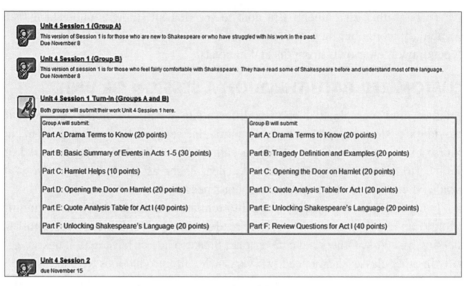

Figure 10.2   Sample Folder Structure

can also be used to help students who have fallen significantly behind get caught up. The unfortunate truth is that, because of a variety of reasons, students will fall behind in your course. They may have health issues, they may struggle with motivation, or they may have low skills. Your challenge will be to help them catch up.

In my school, we use what we call a *critical path* to help students catch up when needed. Basically a critical path is a list of the most critical assignments in any given unit. These are the must-do assignments that you can't let students skip without leaving huge holes in their learning. A student can complete a critical path and get caught up to the rest of the class in a timely manner. It's not ideal but it's one way to help students find success. Following is an example of a critical path for my English 10 course:

Orientation activities under the Unit 1 button: Complete today or tomorrow.

Unit 1 Session 1: Complete the writing territories assignment and the first writing territories journal. Skip everything else. Complete by Wednesday, September 14.

Unit 1 Session 2: Complete the first essay only. Skip everything else. Complete by Friday, September 16.

Unit 1 Session 3: Complete with the class. You should be all caught up at this point!

When I first began teaching online, the idea of using a critical path was distasteful. "Of course it's all important!" I wanted to scream from the rooftops. However, over time I've learned that student success is more important than my pride in my course. I think it would be best if all students completed all assignments in my class. However, if I need to differentiate to meet students' needs and get them caught up, that's something I can do. I want all students to be successful and sometimes that means I need to be flexible.

DIFFERENTIATING FOR SPECIAL NEEDS STUDENTS

Working with special education students is one of the most rewarding and most challenging parts of teaching in an online program. In some ways, the online environment is perfectly suited to the needs of students with individual educational plans (IEPs).

Accommodations for IEP Students

Some very basic accommodations can be quickly and easily supplied to students who have special learning needs in the online environment. The following list is a starting place when you begin working with a student with special needs:

- *Extended time:* Because time is flexible in an online course, special education students can have as much time as they need to grasp concepts without slowing down other students. I've often suspended late penalties and worked with students directly to set reasonable goals for their progress in my class so that they are on a completely separate timetable from other students.

- *Reduced workload:* The online environment is also fairly easy to modify when students need a reduced workload. One easy way to approach this is to take a screenshot of the early screens in a session, one that lists all the work from the session. Then mark up the image to show which assignments you want the student to complete. Students then have clear directions to refer back to as they work through a session.

- *Screen readers:* Online course work is often very text-heavy. For students who struggle with comprehension, this can be a real problem. Thankfully, a screen reader is an easy accommodation that can increase a student's understanding significantly. Software is available that can read an entire screen to students in a clear, crisp voice. Although the reader is still a computerized voice, technology is improving all the time to make those voices understandable and provide the necessary inflection to aid comprehension. Beta versions of Google's browser, Chrome, are even providing a screen reader as a basic option, making a screen reader an excellent accommodation for any student (even those without IEPs).

- *Weekly communication:* Students with IEPs will still need the regular support of a caring adult. One way to make sure they stay in constant contact with you is to require a weekly e-mail on a set day. For example, on Mondays, the teacher e-mails students to update them on what they should be working on that week and any potential challenges. Then, students are required to respond by Tuesday. That way communication lines stay open. It's a great coping strategy that can help IEP students stay connected.

- *Special course assignments:* Because basic course content is usually created before a course begins, it can be hard to make modifications for students who are significantly below grade level. In those cases, students may be assigned to courses below their grade level to better meet their needs. Thankfully, due to the anonymity of the online course environment, there's no stigma in that. A twelve-year-old can take a course alongside a seventeen-year-old and neither one will ever know the difference, while each is getting his needs met.

Challenges

Although there are a lot of accommodations that can be easily provided to special education students, there will still be challenges. Certain learning disabilities require that students have one-on-one support on a regular basis. In those cases, a special education teacher is a critical component of the student's learning plan. That teacher can work directly with the student on a regular basis and help communicate needs to the general education teacher. The special education teacher can monitor course placements and make adjustments as necessary.

Other students may have social-emotional needs that are difficult to support in an online environment. In those cases, it will be crucial to have the support of a school counselor in setting up the student's IEP, goals, and support system.

In addition, it's important for you to be proactive in communicating with all your special needs students (high and low skills). A student may not always reach out for help so it's important for the teacher to initiate the necessary accommodations and stay in touch to see how things are going.

FOCUS ON BLENDED LEARNING

One of the ideas in this chapter involves small group work as a part of a differentiated course. The blended environment is perfect for this kind of group work. Students can work together in the physical classroom to build their initial projects and brainstorm ideas, the kind of messy work that works best when a group is physically together. Then, they can move into the online space for an extended discussion of the topic and for the hard work of putting a project together, with each student building individual components. The strengths of the two environments make for an even better group experience for students.

CHAPTER ELEVEN

GRADING AND FEEDBACK

ESSENTIAL QUESTIONS:

- How is grading different in an online classroom than in a traditional classroom?

- What kind of feedback produces student growth?

- How can I make my grading more efficient as well as effective?

GRADING IN A VIRTUAL SPACE

One of the biggest differences in teaching online versus teaching face-to-face is the grading. Instead of piles of paper spread out behind your desk, you will find green exclamation points or notification icons in your online grade book. You may also find a beautiful list called *needs grading* in your LMS, where you can see every assignment that has been submitted but not graded. Instead of a red pen to mark student mistakes, you'll find a little comment box with space to provide feedback. Or, on some assignments, you'll even find yourself typing within the assignment itself, saving the file, and then returning it to the student. It's a completely different process than grading in a face-to-face classroom. In many ways, it's more efficient but it also requires a completely new skill set.

UNDERSTANDING THE BASICS

The first thing you'll need to grasp is that students in an online classroom submit their work in a completely different way. Each assignment has a Dropbox or assignment submission area where they can turn in their work. Figure 11.1 shows what an assignment looks like in Blackboard.

You can see that there's a space where students can see the point value of the assignment, the due date, and also a space for turning in their work. There's also a button available for attaching a file for the assignment. Figure 11.2 shows what an assignment page looks like in Schoology.

Once a student clicks on "Submit Assignment," they see a screen that looks like figure 11.3.

All LMSs have a similar assignment page with similar features. They should contain a space for uploading a file for the assignment or for copying and pasting their assignment into a submission area. Then, once the assignment is turned in, if students return to that page, they should see a notification that they've already

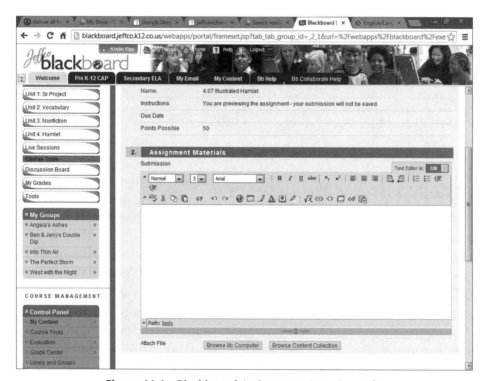

Figure 11.1   Blackboard Assignment Area Example

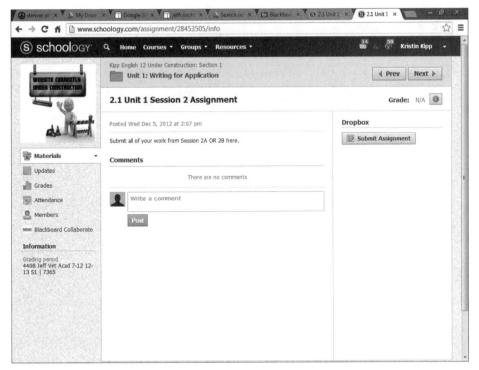

Figure 11.2 Schoology Assignment Area Example

submitted that assignment. In Schoology, the assignment page changes to look like the image in figure 11.4.

That way, students can clearly see that they have submitted the assignment. When enabled, the LMS will also give the student the option to resubmit the assignment if there was a problem or you asked them to redo the work.

The student will also see an indication in the grade book that they have turned in their work. In Blackboard, the indicator is a green exclamation point. All LMSs have some indicator that a student has submitted an assignment. Figure 11.5 shows what our sample student's grades look like after turning in 2.21 Word Log.

The icon that looks like a little blue piece of paper on the top toolbar indicates to the teacher and to the student that the work has been turned in but not graded yet. The teacher sees a similar icon within his or her grade book. The teacher can then go to the assignment and open the file to grade it, as shown in figure 11.6.

The comments on the assignment and the grade can be entered on the same page and then returned to the student. Once that assignment is graded, the grade

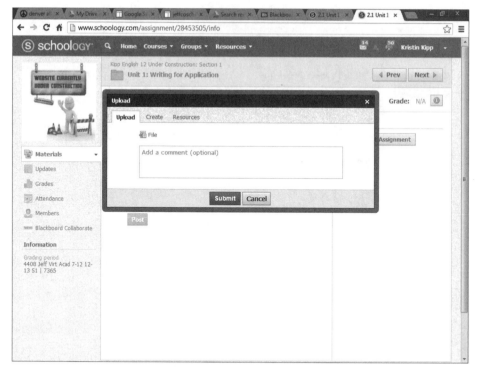

Figure 11.3   Schology Submit Assignment Example

will show up in the student's grade view along with the teacher's feedback, as shown in figure 11.7.

You can see how the LMS changes the grading process dramatically! A student can easily submit work in a file and the teacher can easily grade it. Comments on those assignments are immediately returned to students in their grade book so they have a real understanding of their progress at any time.

Although grading from within a LMS can be far more efficient than the old system of passing back and forth hard copy papers, it can also be a challenge. In the past, you may have had several assignments that were returned to students without comments. Then you shared your overall feedback with the entire class the next time you were together. You may also have given students completion grades on some assignments and, again, didn't provide comments. In an online course, those comments are a critical line of communication between you and the students. It will be vital that you provide feedback on as many assignments as possible so that when students click on the grades button in your LMS, they see a detailed list of grades with comments explaining how they can improve. In the

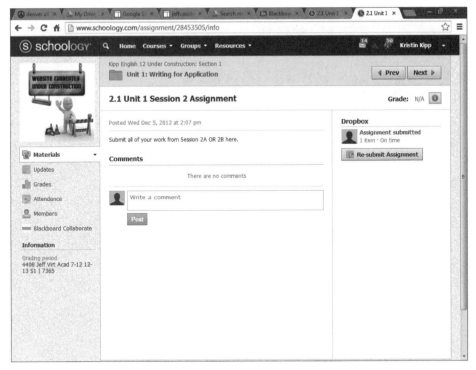

Figure 11.4   Schoology Submitted Assignment Example

rest of this chapter, we'll explore how to provide that feedback in an efficient way that helps students grow.

CANNED COMMENTS AND PERSONALIZING FEEDBACK

The idea of providing comments on every assignment for every student can get to be a bit overwhelming. Thankfully there are some relatively simple tricks that can speed up the process. One way to provide detailed feedback efficiently is the use of canned comments. Canned comments have gotten a bad name because they're obviously not personalized for every student but they can be a necessary evil when you want all students to receive feedback but there's not time to personalize every comment. There are several ways to tackle this that are still ethical and personal.

The first way to provide canned comments is to give the exact same comments for every student. This works best for an assignment in which everyone is receiving a completion score or you want everyone to receive the same feedback

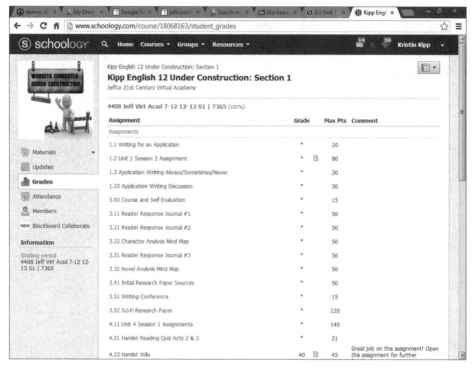

Figure 11.5   Sample Student Grade View Schoology

Figure 11.6   Sample Student Grade in Schoology Gradebook

highlighting one particular point. For example, I might provide everyone with a comment like this:

> *Assignment 2.3 is a completion score and you've earned full credit. Remember to use the key points from this assignment as you start tackling our final project!*

Students are still receiving helpful reminders about their progress and where they should be focused but those reminders are the same for every student. The teacher can just copy and paste the exact same verbiage in every student's

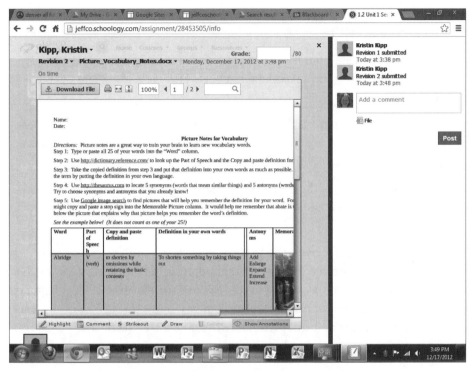

Figure 11.7 Sample Graded Assignment in Schoology

assignment and assign a score. For students who severely missed the mark on the assignment, the feedback might be more personalized but the general feedback might work for most students. This type of feedback should be used sparingly because it's obvious to students that it was not customized for their work. However, it can be a nice time-saver for assignments that don't require in-depth feedback.

Another more personalized way to use canned comments is to create a set of six to ten different comments when you first begin grading an assignment (or as you grade the first few submissions). This set of comments is reflective of the types of errors you might expect on that particular assignment. Then you can pick and choose from the list of comments based on how a student performed on the assignment. Here's an example comment set from a short-answer assignment:

- Great work! I appreciate that you added so many details from the story in your answer.

- Be careful of run-on sentences. To fix them, combine with a conjunction and a comma, add a semicolon, or split the sentence into two different sentences.

- I would have liked to see more evidence in your responses. Remember that every opinion must be supported by facts!

- This was a great start but it's incomplete. Just answering the question isn't enough. I'd like to see you explain your answers and justify them with evidence.

- For your next assignment, I'd like you to start experimenting with the length of your sentences. Using some short sentences and some long sentences is a great way to give your writing a more natural feel.

- You missed several of these questions. Please come by office hours to chat with me about it and redo the assignment.

Each student then receives one to three comments on their assignment. You can just copy and paste the statements that apply to the work. If none of them apply, you might type up a personalized response for that particular assignment but for the most part you should be able to quickly move through the work using your canned comments and still give students personalized feedback.

Here's another set of canned comments, in this case for an essay:

Commended Skills

I love how you used so many quotations from the play to support your main ideas. It made your argument far stronger.

Great job coming up with an interesting, arguable thesis statement. Coming up with a good topic is half the battle in an essay like this!

I like how you organized this essay. I could tell what the focus of each paragraph was and it made it much easier to read.

I like your writing voice. Even though you were writing about literature, it was a really natural style that was interesting to read.

I loved your word choice! Keep experimenting with language to make your writing interesting.

Great job with sentence fluency! You worked in a lot of quotations from the play in a way that was really natural and read easily.

Excellent job with your conclusion and explaining Wilde's larger point in the play.

Great job creating a simple, arguable thesis and then proving it with quotes from the play. What a great start in learning how to write a literary analysis paper!

Skills to Work On

I want you to focus on elaboration. For an essay like this, it was absolutely vital to include a lot of quotations from the play and a lot of specific examples. Without that, the argument is weak. For any essay, the more specific you are with examples, quotes, reasons, and statistics, the stronger your argument will be.

I want you to work on making your writing sound more natural. You should be able to read it out loud without tripping over any phrases. If it's hard for you to read out loud, it will be hard for someone else to read, too!

Focus on editing. There are a few strategies you can try. One is to work with a friend or an adult (even a teacher!) who is a good editor. Have that person read your essay with you and point out errors. Then you can correct them. Another option is to use the spell-check and grammar check on your word processor. It can help a lot! Grammarly.com is also a great resource for revision.

You should think about how to weave in your sources and quotations without it sounding awkward. Here's a resource that can help: *Using Quotations* (www.adlc.ca/index2.php?option=com_docman&task=doc_view&gid =500&Itemid=138).

In an essay like this, you're trying to accomplish two things: (1) You want to prove your thesis using a lot of quotes from the play. (2) You want to back up to the big picture and explain what Wilde's greater point about humanity is. You did a great job with the first point but I would have liked to see more analysis around what Wilde's larger point was.

You also had quite a few run-ons in this essay. Here's a resource that can help: *Run-On Sentences, Comma Splices* (http://grammar.ccc.commnet.edu/ grammar/runons.htm).

I want you to focus on avoiding wordy sentences. You always want to explain your ideas in the simplest way possible so that they're clear to the reader.

Also, be careful of repeating yourself too often. Saying something once is usually enough ☺.

Also, in this essay you didn't always provide enough background information for your readers so they know where you're headed. In a literary analysis essay, assume readers have read the play but it's been a while. They need a bit of explanation to be able to follow where you are in the play and what point you're making.

I want you to start experimenting with language. There are times when it's best to use sophisticated, complicated language and there are times when it's best to just say something simply. Start playing with both styles and seeing when it's more effective to be simple. Also, try using some figurative language in your writing.

I want you to work on writing introductions. They should interest the reader without too much detail and without too much repetition. Here's a resource that can help: *Introductions* (http://writingcenter.unc.edu/handouts/introductions).

The comments are more in-depth because the assignment is a full essay. Each student might receive three or four of the comments, customized for his or her needs.

The final way you can use canned comments to speed up your grading is to use half-canned comments and half-personalized comments on any given assignment. As in the previous example, you might start with six to ten canned comments that you plan to use on an assignment. Then you'll copy and paste the ones that apply for a particular student. But, in order to provide a more personalized feel, you might add one sentence at the start of the feedback that includes the student's name and a brief statement of how he or she did. For example, you might add, "Kaitlyn, nice work on this" or "Jennifer, I was hoping for more on this assignment." From there you can add in the canned comments. Then, at the end, you might add another sentence or two that references a specific sentence or idea in the student's work and how it contributed to the overall quality of the work. Again, you're using canned comments to speed up the grading process but you're also letting students know that you've read their individual assignments and that you care about their success. Here's what the final product might look like, with the canned portions in italics:

> Jennifer, *I was hoping for more on this assignment.* This was a great start but it's incomplete. Just answering the question isn't enough. I'd like to see you explain your answers and justify them with evidence. *I really liked what you put about Lincoln and his plans for the future. I just need to see those ideas fleshed out more!*

Although canned comments can be a time-saver, some assignments are so important that no canned comments should be used at all. Instead, you'll just need to plan time to provide personalized feedback to each student. In that case, it's helpful to think of your comments in terms of positives and negatives. First, provide the student with at least one positive thing from his or her work. Then, provide an area that needs improvement and some encouragement to work on that issue in the next assignment. Students will appreciate that you've taken the time to customize their feedback and, if you write the feedback well, they'll also quickly learn that you care deeply about their success.

RUBRIC GRADING

Another way you can speed up your grading is by using well-created rubrics as much as possible. A well-created rubric will not only let students know how they did on an assignment but it will also give them ideas for how to improve in the future. Here's a rubric I use regularly with reader response journals:

A = 45–50 points

Reader response journal is thorough and thoughtful as well as being written in clear sentences and paragraphs. Student reflects on this quarter of the book in a critical way that shows me they're reading *and* thinking deeply about the content. Student includes specific events from the text and quotations to prove his or her points. Future attempts should keep up this level of analysis, even taking it deeper when possible.

B = 40–44 points

Reader response journal shows that the student read this quarter of the book. The student also includes some analysis of the story. May include limited grammatical or organizational errors. Future attempts should focus on taking that analysis to a deeper level using quotations or specific events from the book.

C = 35–39 points

Reader response journal shows that the student read this quarter of the book. May fall back on writing a summary with limited to no analysis of the story. May also have some grammatical or organizational errors. Future attempts should focus on going beyond a summary of the book to including the reader's thoughts about the story. Future attempts should also focus on writing in clear, cohesive paragraphs and sentences.

D = 30–34 points

Reader response journal does not prove the student read this quarter of the book. There is not enough detail provided. May also have significant grammatical or organizational errors. Future attempts should focus on including lots of information from the book as well as analysis of the storyline.

F = less than 30 points

Does not meet the minimum requirements for the assignment: minimum of one page in length, discusses (not summarizes) events from the entire quarter of the book, demonstrates critical thinking about the novel, written in cohesive paragraphs with clear topic sentences. Future attempts should focus on meeting the minimum requirements. May resubmit for more points.

When I'm grading journals, I provide personalized feedback to students first, including referring to a specific portion of their journals that I appreciated or had questions about. Then I copy and paste the portion of the rubric that applies to their assignment. That way they know which score they earned and also have some feedback about how to improve on the next journal. This is particularly important for an assignment in which students will be doing a similar task several times during the semester.

This kind of rubric is a holistic rubric. Students are basically sorted into five categories based on letter grade and then I have some flexibility to assign a grade within that letter grade, indicating whether the score was close to the next letter grade, squarely in the middle, or almost one category further down.

On larger assignments and projects, instead of a holistic rubric, I use a rubric with several different categories in a table. That way students are receiving even more detailed feedback about their performance in different areas. In some LMSs, such as Blackboard, you'll even be able to input your rubric right into the LMS and fill it out in the system.

I have a favorite six traits rubric that I use regularly. Using that rubric, I can quickly highlight which category applies to the student's work for each of the six traits, type in a few helpful comments, and copy and paste the whole thing into my LMS. Students appreciate the detailed feedback and having that rubric ahead of time to prepare.

The real key is to remember that using a rubric in an online course not only speeds up grading but also provides students with more real-time feedback on how to improve.

WORD OPTIONS FOR GRADING STUDENT WORK

In addition to providing canned comments or a rubric for each student's assignments, you'll also want to explore downloading a student's file and providing comments right in the assignment itself. There's really no substitute for receiving feedback right within the original assignment so you'll want to do that when detailed feedback is key.

Microsoft Word provides some great options for marking up student work. In Word 2010, the review tab offers the option to add comments to a file. You can add comments throughout a student's assignment, save the file, and then return it to the student. When it's done the complete file with comments looks something like figure 11.8. This function is also available in other versions of Word.

In general, when I'm providing detailed feedback like this, I download the file to my hard drive, add my comments, and then save as a pdf. Providing the file as a pdf rather than a Word document ensures the security of the grading rubric

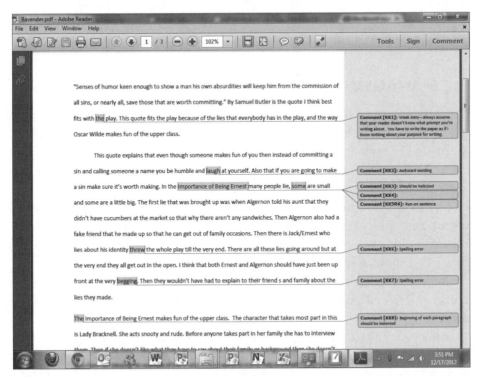

Figure 11.8 Sample Student Work with Teacher Comments Using Word's Comment Feature

on the assignment feedback but also encourages students to make their revisions manually within Word (rather than just ''accepting'' my suggested revisions), a powerful learning experience for their writing. Then the pdf gets loaded back into my LMS and I tell the student to see the attachment. Although there are a few more steps involved in this sort of grading, it can be very helpful for students.

Another way to do this kind of detailed feedback more efficiently is to create a macro in Microsoft Word. A macro is a series of commonly used keystrokes that you have your computer memorize. Then, instead of entering that set of keystrokes, you push the button for your macro and they all come up at once. For example, in my grading I find myself adding a comment and entering ''Run-on sentence. Please revise.'' over and over again. To speed up that work, I've created a run-on macro. When I come across a run-on in a student's work, I put the cursor at the end of the sentence and hit my run-on button. A comment box will automatically pop up to the side of the assignment with the text, ''Run-on sentence. Please revise.'' in it. Instead of typing the entire phrase, I've only had to push one button. Using macros can be a very effective way of speeding up your grading. You can find the options for creating a macro in Word under the ''View'' menu. There are also multiple tutorials on how to set up macros if you perform a quick search in YouTube.

FILE MANAGEMENT

The end result of all of this electronic grading is that you will have a lot of files moving back and forth from your hard drive. Having an efficient file management system will be essential. On my computer, I have a folder for each of the classes I teach. Then, within that folder, there's another layer of folders for the units in that course. Inside each unit folder is a folder for various assignments. Each year I start with a new file structure. At the end of that year, I rename the folder ''Archive School Year 20xx–20xx.'' Although having all those layers of folders can be frustrating, I know where everything is and how to find the files I need quickly. Figure 11.9 shows a screenshot of what that file system looks like.

Believe me, staying organized will be critical to your success as an online teacher. A basic file system on your computer will help to keep everything in its place.

Although the prospect of grading everything online can be a bit daunting, as you become accustomed to your new system, it will become second nature. You'll eventually find that you're much faster at grading within your LMS and students are receiving far better feedback than you were ever able to provide on a hard copy. Everyone wins!

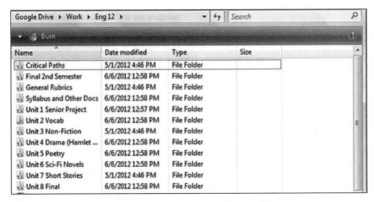

Figure 11.9 Screenshot of Sample File Management System

Interview with Anthony Launey, IDEAL New Mexico

Teacher Anthony Launey is fully convinced that online learning is the way of the future. He personally experiences kids who "just wouldn't get math any other way" and he's excited to be a part of the movement. Launey teaches statistics for IDEAL New Mexico, a state-run virtual program. Through his online statistics course, he's able to reach students who otherwise would never have the opportunity to take statistics. Finding a qualified statistics teacher in a rural area can be a significant challenge. Instead, schools contract through IDEAL New Mexico and have their students take statistics with Launey.

Launey says that teaching math online is significantly different than in a classroom. For one, it's hard for students to show their work. Instead, Launey has them write out an explanation for how they came to the correct answer. That way, he can understand their thinking and he can usually diagnose any problems from their written explanation. In some ways, their demonstration of understanding is much more sophisticated than just working out the problem. Then, he's able to provide personalized feedback on every assignment to help the student improve.

Launey says that one of the best parts of online learning is the wealth of resources that are available. He can bring the best instruction possible to his students via Kahn Academy and other online video tools. "These skilled communicators may be better at this than 90 percent of the teachers in a classroom and I can share their work with my students," says Launey. Launey even uses those resources to provide detailed feedback on an assignment. When it becomes clear from a particular assignment that a student is struggling with a concept, Launey can do a quick search for a video that explains that concept. Then, students receive a link to that video in their assignment feedback. It's a powerful way to help student improve their work. Even better? Launey teaches his students how to search Google or the Kahn Academy website to find the specific video that meets their needs. By the end of the course, they are able to answer many of their own questions.

By taking the time to provide personalized feedback that often includes outside resources, Launey is seeing significant improvements in student achievement and a better learning environment overall.

FOCUS ON BLENDED LEARNING

In your blended classroom, you'll want to consider using an online grade book for all your assignments, not just the ones in the online portion of your course. Features such as an online Dropbox, file management, and custom feedback make an online grade book significantly more efficient than traditional methods. Also, using the strategies in this chapter, students will receive more feedback on their assignments.

The first step in implementing online grading is to introduce the Dropbox feature of your LMS to students. This should be done in the face-to-face portion of the course so you can demonstrate the tool to students and they can ask real-time questions. Then, you can send students home to submit their first assignments. After the first assignment is due and you've returned the work to students, take the time to demonstrate how to find your feedback within the LMS. That feedback is critical to your student's success in the online course environment so it's important that they're checking the comments regularly and adjusting their work accordingly. It's worth taking the time in class to show them how to find the feedback because some LMSs tend to hide feedback under several screen clicks. You may even want to consider recording a video on how to find feedback and posting it prominently in the online portion of your course.

You may be tempted to provide only limited feedback on assignments within your online system and instead give feedback to the whole class when you see them face-to-face. It's important to avoid that temptation. Students need personal feedback that they can refer to on a regular basis and reread when needed. That feedback is best provided in the online environment rather than during a face-to-face lecture. Many students aren't good listeners face-to-face and your feedback won't be as effective that way, even if it is sometimes more expedient.

CHAPTER TWELVE

ACCESSIBILITY, COMMUNICATION, AND OFFICE HOURS

ESSENTIAL QUESTIONS:

- How can I make myself available to my students?

- What forms of communication are most effective with students?

- What do office hours look like in a virtual space?

- How can I safely text with students?

COMMUNICATING WITH DIGITAL NATIVES: SPEAKING THEIR LANGUAGE

One of the greatest challenges of living fully in a digital space is that all of your communications live in that space, too. From IM to phone calls to text messages and e-mails, you have to find a way to communicate who you are to your students. They need to know that you care about them and want their success and it all has to be done at a distance. That can be a challenge!

What's amazing is that once you overcome those obstacles you will get to know your students very deeply, sometimes more than you would have if you'd had those same students in a face-to-face classroom. It's hard to believe what students will share with you via a text message or an e-mail when you take the time to let them know you care. Kids need caring adults in their lives and that's why it's absolutely vital to find ways to communicate effectively.

In this chapter we'll explore a variety of strategies for effectively communicating with students. Before we begin though, it's prudent to take a moment and think about communication styles. Every person has a preferred mode of digital communication. Some people like to e-mail about everything, even something as simple as setting up a doctor's appointment. Others prefer a phone call. They miss the ''real'' interaction when doing business. Many of your students will prefer text messaging. It's a very comfortable medium for them and thus it's often how they like to communicate with their teachers as well as their friends. You probably have a very clear preference also. For me, it's e-mail. I love e-mail and use it for everything. However, as an online teacher, you will often have to set aside your preferred communication method in order to meet the needs of your students. Although e-mail is my preference, every day I communicate with students via texting, IM, phone calls, and even Skype. Meeting students' needs often means matching their communication style.

Think of it this way: You are an ambassador for your students, helping them to cross the border into a foreign environment, your content area. As an ambassador, you have to be multilingual, communicating in all different forms, to make sure that your immigrants feel comfortable. When you have a student whose primary language is text messaging, you'll speak ''texting'' for them so they feel comfortable in your virtual space and in having a relationship with their virtual teacher. When you have a student whose primary language is a phone call, you'll make that adjustment, too. Part of the online teacher's job is to bridge that divide for all students.

Last semester I had an eye-opening experience that helped me to come to terms with this exact issue. In my course survey at the beginning of my course, I have a question that asks students to provide an e-mail address that they will check daily during of the class. Because my primary communication method is e-mail, I use e-mail quite a bit to communicate basic course information to students. One of my students replied on that initial survey that she was giving me an e-mail address but she rarely, if ever, would check that e-mail address. Instead, she requested that I put all e-mails into a text message to her so she didn't miss anything. In fact she said, ''I hate computers and try to avoid them at all costs. Texting is really the best way to reach me.''

My first reaction was disbelief. How could a student sign up for an online course and hate computers? How could she *never* check e-mail and hope to be successful in an online class? Once I calmed down, I realized that this was a student who needed me to reach out. She wouldn't be successful in an online course if she never went near a computer. My job was to bridge the gap. If I could find a way to engage this student in regular text messages with me, she might just get engaged with my course content and become more comfortable using a computer to learn the content she needed. I researched some ways to get my course e-mails delivered as text messages to the student and she was immensely grateful. (There's more information on how to do that later in this chapter.) Through some minor adjustments on my part, I was able to reach a student who otherwise probably would have failed in my class. Instead, she successfully completed the course and, at least in some ways, overcame her fear of computers. Being that ambassador for your students by using their preferred communication method is absolutely vital. It's not just a luxury. For some students, it will mean the difference between failing the course altogether or having a successful learning experience.

OFFICE HOURS AND TUTORING

One of the most tangible ways you can be available for your students is to set some basic office hours for your course. Office hours in the virtual world are a set time when you commit to always being available for students to contact you. I tell students that during my set office hours they will never have to leave a voicemail or wait for a response on e-mail. All e-mails received during that time will be immediately returned and all phone calls will be answered. Students appreciate knowing that you're available to them in real time and they'll come to rely on office hours to get questions answered and to get additional help.

In my school, we take the additional step of having a synchronous session open and available during a teacher's office hours. That way students can not only call or e-mail during that time and get an immediate answer but they can also come to a live session and see their teacher. This type of interaction is particularly helpful for having a video chat and screen sharing. If I can see a student's screen while they're explaining a problem to me, it's easier for me to help them troubleshoot. Those synchronous sessions are just one more line of communication that I want to keep open for students.

Setting Times for Office Hours

You'll want to host some sort of office hours three to four hours per week. A student should be able to look at the course calendar and see an office hours session is coming up within a day or two of any point in the course. That way, if a live interaction is necessary, a student will never have to wait very long to see you.

You'll also want to consider hosting office hours at several different times of day. Some students may only be available in the afternoon. Others will need a morning option. It's important to maintain that flexibility. I always host an office hours session on the evening of a day that an assignment is due. Unfortunately, students tend to procrastinate and I can anticipate 50 percent of my class will be working on their assignment on the evening of my latest due date! I want to make sure I'm available and thus I make hosting that evening office hours session a priority. It's by far my best-attended session.

Inviting Students to Office Hours

Although being available to your students during office hours is important, unfortunately it's not enough. Some students will still be too intimidated to show up during office hours or scared to ask for your help during that time. Instead, you'll need to go out of your way to invite particular students to visit with you during office hours. Students whom you notice are not getting the content or are falling behind should receive a personal invitation from you to come by during office hours. That invitation should include a link to a synchronous session if that's the way you host your help sessions. That way you're making attendance as easy as possible. I've even experimented with making attendance at an office hours session a part of a student's grade. For example, students might have to come by my office hours sometime during the month of October for a mid-term conference. They then receive a participation grade for touching base with me. Those invitations and even grades can be a big motivator to help students feel comfortable with you and comfortable using your office hours sessions.

A Disclaimer about Office Hours

Although office hours can be an extremely valuable part of your course, try not to panic if students don't attend office hours regularly. That's a usual part of the ebb and flow of a course. At times, you'll have quite a few students coming by office hours. At other times, you may have none at all. The reasons for that are several. For one, students just may not need your help during office hours if they are progressing well through the course already. That's a good thing! It means that your course is structured well and students are not having trouble with the content. Another reason that students may not come by office hours is that they're communicating with you in other ways instead. If an e-mail is always returned within an hour or two, they don't have a reason to come by office hours. Their questions are already being answered. That's OK, too.

Even if you find that your office hours sessions are not being used regularly, it's still important to have them available to students. You never know when that one student might drop by who won't contact you in any other way. Having office hours available and knowing that they're not ''bothering'' you during that time could be just the motivation they need to reconnect with your class.

Small-Group Tutoring Sessions

Another way you might use a synchronous tool to connect with your students is to offer a small-group tutoring session. For example, a math teacher might find that the majority of her students don't understand fractions. Although fractions aren't a part of the year's curriculum, that teacher could offer a small-group tutoring session just for those students who are struggling. Then she could require that particular students attend that session or watch the recording. This can be a powerful way to meet the needs of all students, especially those who are struggling. Alternatively, the teacher could make the session optional and record it as a reference for future students needing additional instruction.

Whole-Class Optional Tutoring Sessions

Along the same lines, you might want to consider offering a whole-class tutoring session via a synchronous tool. If the majority of the class is struggling with a particular concept, you can set up a tutoring session and send an invitation to all the students in your class. The session is optional so that students who can't attend won't be punished but you can also record the session so anyone can watch it later if they find they're struggling. What an amazing resource to have available! Imagine a student e-mailing you because he's struggling with a concept and being able to refer him to a particular tutoring session recording in which you went over that exact assignment and topic. The results are powerful, personalized, just-in-time learning.

COMMUNICATION METHODS

Although office hours, tutoring, and synchronous sessions can be powerful tools, the majority of your communications will probably happen in other avenues in which you're reaching out to students via e-mailing, texting, IM, or phone.

E-mail

E-mail will probably be one of the primary communication methods in your course. Students and teachers are comfortable using e-mail and it can be a great way to keep students connected. E-mail can be a powerful tool to use with students but only if you train them to use it regularly and responsibly. A recent survey by Pew

Internet Research shows that only 11 percent of teens use e-mail daily and the numbers are declining each year (Lenhart, Ling, Campbell, & Purcell, 2010). If you expect your students to automatically check e-mail daily, you'll probably be disappointed. If you let students know that you expect them to check e-mail daily and respond to messages within twenty-four hours, many students will comply but not all. However, you can change their behavior by making e-mail communications a required part of your course. Even when you do make e-mail a requirement, you'll want to also use other methods when you find students are not responding to you via e-mail (especially if nine out of ten of them are not checking their e-mail daily when they start your course!).

That being said, e-mail can still be a powerful tool. Because an e-mail is not limited by length considerations (like texting, tweeting, or IM might be), it can be a great place to communicate detailed information to your students. If your students are checking e-mail regularly, it can also be a great place to provide encouragement and answer questions.

E-mail Distribution Lists   One of the first things you'll want to do each semester is to set up a contact list in your e-mail program that includes all of your students and their current e-mail addresses. As a bonus, you might even want to include a separate list of their parent's e-mail addresses. You can then use those contact lists to set up a distribution list for the class and for parents. All e-mail programs have some method of setting up a list or group so that you can simply type in the name of the list and all the e-mail addresses from that list will automatically be loaded. That distribution list can be accessed with just a few key strokes and you can e-mail your entire class quickly and easily. It can be a great way to send regular updates outside the LMS. Announcements within the system are great but they only work if a student has logged in to work on your course anyway. For many students, receiving an e-mail reminder of a due date is a great way to remind them to log in and get to work!

When using a distribution list, it's absolutely vital that you remember to enter the distribution list in the "bcc" section of your e-mail instead of the "to" or "cc" sections. That way student's e-mail addresses remain confidential because everyone receives a blind carbon copy of the e-mail. The last thing you want to do is have a student e-mail the entire class something inappropriate. By using bcc you're making sure they don't have that access.

E-mail Routines: Six Weekly E-mails That Make a Difference   Once you have your distribution lists set up, your next step will be to begin using e-mail as a part of your weekly routine. In my workflow, I've discovered six different types of e-mails that I try to send regularly. I simply add these to my to-do list on different days of the week to make sure that students who need them are getting these e-mails regularly.

- *Beginning-of-the-week e-mail:* The first type of e-mail I send regularly is one that goes to all students in a particular class at the beginning of the week. This is an e-mail I send to remind student that we're starting a new session and encourage them to get started. Following is an example of what this e-mail looks like:
  - Hi everyone! Happy Wednesday! This is just a reminder that today is the start of a new week in English 10. You should be working on Unit 8 Session 4. It'll be due next Tuesday. Let me know if you have any questions. I'm here to help!—Ms. Kipp

- *Reminder e-mail:* The second type of e-mail I send regularly is a due date reminder e-mail. This is sent either the day of a deadline or the night before. It's basically just one more reminder that the student has something due. Again, if students have not logged in recently, they might have missed that they have a deadline. Like the new week e-mail, this e-mail is sent to the entire class. Following is an example of what this e-mail looks like:
  - Good evening! Please don't forget that Unit 8 Session 4 is due tomorrow. If you're getting stuck on the imagery assignment, be sure you watch the live session. We even did some example questions together! Let me know if you need help. ☺—Ms. Kipp

- *Touch-base e-mail:* The next type of e-mail I send regularly is a touch-base e-mail. Unlike the first two e-mails listed here, this one is sent only to particular students. These students are those in the 60 to 80 percent grade range in my class, students who might not reach out to me if I didn't initiate the conversation. You'll be amazed how many of these students will respond with questions they have about class! They wouldn't reach out to you with that question usually but if you contact them, they appreciate the opportunity to ask a question. I tend to send this type of e-mail to six to ten students each week. Following is an example:
  - Hi [insert student's name]! I just wanted to make sure everything is going OK for you in class. Let me know if you have any questions or need help!—Ms. Kipp

- *Way-to-go e-mail:* Similar to the touch-base e-mail, the way-to-go e-mail is sent to a select group of students each week. These are students in the 85 to 100 percent grade range who are really doing well in my course. They can also be students who have made significant improvement in the last week (such as a grade change of 5 percent or more). I send these grade change e-mails even if the percentage change is just from a 20 percent to a 25 percent. Students need as much positive feedback as possible and a quick e-mail of congratulations can make a huge difference. I try to send six to ten of these each week. Here's an example for an ''A'' student and for a student with a grade change:

  - Hi [insert student name]! You're doing awesome in class. Congratulations on keeping that A! Keep up the good work and let me know if you have any questions.—Ms. Kipp

  - Hi [insert student name]! I noticed that your grade went up some this week. Great job! Keep going and let me know if you have questions!—Ms. Kipp

- *Struggling student e-mail:* The struggling student e-mail is one of my many attempts to reengage students who are not performing well in class. I use it for any student in the 0 to 59 percent grade range (because 60 percent is passing in my class). I have different variations that I send to students. Because they will get this e-mail every two weeks or so until they get their grade up, it's important that it's not repetitive! Here are some examples of how to word this tricky e-mail:

  - Hi [insert student name]. I'm worried about your progress in class. What's up?—Ms. Kipp

  - Hi [insert student name]. I noticed that your grade dropped quite a bit this week. Is everything OK? Let me know if you have questions.—Ms. Kipp

  - Hi [insert student name]. Remember that English is a requirement for graduation! I really want to help you get this grade up. Please give me a call and we can talk options, [insert phone number].—Ms. Kipp

  - Hey [insert student name]. I'm having office hours this Tuesday from 5–7 P.M. Can you stop by and we can talk about your grade and how to get it back up? The link to attend is down below in my e-mail signature.—Ms. Kipp

- *Attendance e-mail:* Similar to the struggling student e-mail, the attendance e-mail is an opportunity to reengage a student who has checked out of the course and stopped attending. Unlike the other e-mails listed, this e-mail is based on a student's log-in history rather than his or her overall grade. Here's an example:

- Hi [insert student name]. I noticed that the last time you logged in was February 12. Remember that daily attendance is a requirement of the class and of the school. Let me know if you're having trouble accessing the course. I'm happy to help. —Ms. Kipp

At first glance, these e-mails may seem a bit prescriptive. Although it's not necessary to use this exact language in your e-mails with students, it is important that you're using all six types of messages somewhere in your daily routine. Students need personal contact from you and creating a routine for those contacts can be extremely helpful. For example, I know that if it's Tuesday, I need to send six to ten way-to-go e-mails. If that were not part of my regular routine and workflow, I might easily skip those e-mails and miss out on an opportunity to engage my students.

Texting: The Secret Weapon

In addition to e-mail, you'll want to include text messaging as a regular part of your communication routine. The same Pew survey that found that only 11 percent of teens use e-mails daily showed that 72 percent of teens ages twelve to seventeen send and receive text messages every day. In fact, an average teen sends at least fifty texts every day (Lenhart, Ling, Campbell, & Purcell, 2010). If you begin to text with your students, you'll find that it's a powerful medium for engaging them in learning.

Many teachers have steered clear of using text messages because of fears over safety. There have been entirely too many headlines that showcased a teacher sending inappropriate texts to a minor. However, just because some teachers have used text messaging inappropriately doesn't mean that we should stop using it completely. There are some powerful benefits to texting with students, especially for an online teacher. Those benefits far outweigh the risks, especially when there are some very basic things that teachers can do to mitigate those risks.

Any time a teacher texts with a student, three overarching principles should always be in place:

- There should be a clear, easily accessed *record of all text messages* sent and received from a particular account. I use Google Voice for that purpose, ensuring that if there were ever any doubt about the texts that were sent and received, I have a clear record (more on that on the following page).

- Any communications sent via text messaging should still be *professional and appropriate*, including correct grammar! Students should realize that you're using text messaging as a professional communication. When they realize that, they'll usually reciprocate and keep everything "school appropriate."

- Finally, if any message starts to get emotional, for example if a student is clearly upset with you or if the conversation starts to get complicated, follow up the text message with a phone call. It's better to clear the air and discuss more complicated issues via a phone call. There's less room for misunderstandings.

Using Google Voice   One of the easiest ways to text message with students in a way that has a permanent, easily accessible record is to use Google Voice, which is a free tool created by Google to be a central hub for your telephone and text messaging interactions. Basically, Google assigns you an alternate phone number. Then, any time someone calls that number, you can have Google forward that call to any phone you choose. When you're at home, the call might forward to a land line. When you're on the go, the call might forward to your cell phone. It could even forward to several phones at once and you can answer wherever is most convenient.

For texting, the real bonus to using Google Voice is that there's an online interface for sending text messages. Instead of typing on the tiny keyboard on your phone, you can send and receive text messages right from the online interface in your web browser. If you're sending the same message several times, you can copy and paste that message as needed.

Google Voice also leaves behind a great archive of all your communications with a student. All text messages and voicemails are saved and can be searched. You can find any conversation with any student by typing in the student's name or a keyword. If needed, you could easily find every message ever sent between a teacher and a student.

In addition to sending and receiving text messages via Google Voice, you can also use the tool as your voicemail. All voicemails are automatically transcribed into text once they are received. Although the transcription technology is not perfect, it can be a great way to quickly see the gist of a message and handle it appropriately. It also saves a lot of time listening to messages!

Using Text for the Most Vital Messages   Regardless of whether you're using Google Voice or another system for sending and receiving text messages with students, you'll want to think about how to use texts most effectively. In my practice, I use text messages for only the most vital communications. I realize how powerful the medium is and I don't want to overuse it by flooding students with messages. In general, a student might receive two or three texts from me during a given month and only if needed. That being said, texting is extremely powerful. Even students who never respond to e-mails or answer phone calls will usually text message me if I contact them in a friendly, respectful way. I use that to my advantage as much as possible!

E-mail-to-Text Options   Although I text individual students only on an as-needed basis for the most vital messages, I do give students the option to receive my class e-mails as text messages. For students who don't (or won't!) check e-mail, this is a good option. Any texting phone number can be translated into an e-mail address. So a phone number of 999-888-7777 with Verizon as the carrier will become 9998887777@vtext.com. If I add that e-mail address to my distribution list, students will receive a text message that includes the first 160 character of my e-mail any time I send an e-mail to that address, which includes any time I e-mail the entire class. Those 160 characters may not be enough for them to get my entire message but it will be a reminder for them to check their e-mail. The Email Text Messages website (www.emailtextmessages.com) has a complete list of different carriers and how to translate a phone number with that carrier into an e-mail address. Again, I provide this as an option for students but I don't do it for everyone because I don't want to flood their text in-boxes and make the medium less effective.

Setting Parameters for Response Times   One of the real issues you'll have to face once you start texting with students is that at first they may not understand your boundaries on text messages. It's not at all uncommon for a student to text at 10 P.M. and hope for a response that night. As the teacher of the course, it'll be important to communicate expectations with your students of when you will and will not answer texts (and e-mails and phone calls, too). I generally tell students that I'm available Monday through Friday between 8 A.M. and 6 P.M. Outside of that time, I'm not available because I'm spending time with my family. I explain that I'll answer their messages by the next day but I can't be available 24–7 without burning out. Once you've set that expectation, your students will probably still text at 10 P.M. but they won't be disappointed when you don't answer until the next morning!

All in all, texting is an absolutely fabulous tool for working with students. It's a communication method that most teens use on a daily basis and they'll appreciate you're speaking their language. Texting can become a secret weapon to engage even the most reluctant learner.

IM: The Always on Tool

In addition to e-mail and texting, you may also want to include IM in your communication arsenal. Windows, Google, Yahoo!, and AOL all provide viable options and many of them will work together. An IM program simply provides an option for letting your students (and coworkers) know that you're online and available to chat. Then, when someone has a quick question, they can send you an IM and get an instant response. Some students will use IM regularly to ask questions while they're working on assignments.

My experience has been that not many students use IM regularly. However, I always have a group of five to ten students each semester who use the medium all the time. They like the right-there feeling and knowing that help is on call whenever they need it. I ask every student to sign up for an IM account and add me to their ''Friends'' list at the beginning of the semester but I don't require that they use the tool unless they find it's helpful. For those who do use it, it's a lifeline and it's one I want to continue to offer them if they need it.

You'll want to talk to the rest of your school about which IM program to use. Any one will work just fine but you'll want a consistent tool with the other teachers in your program so that it's easy for students to contact anyone in the organization. Then, that tool should be taught in all their classes and reinforced as an option.

On a side note, you may also find that IM is a great tool for staff and community development. When all your teachers are online each day, even if they're working from home, you'll find that a just-down-the-hall feeling develops. Teachers can use IM to ask questions of each other and troubleshoot at a moment's notice. It's a great way to create community!

Phone Calls: Going Old Fashioned

Although all the tools listed in this chapter will be important in your communications with students, having an actual voice interaction is, at times, critical. You'll want to make sure your phone number is posted visibly in your course and that students are encouraged to contact you on the phone. They should feel comfortable with calling you and you should reassure them that it's never a bother to talk on the phone.

You'll also want to reach out to students who are struggling via a phone call. A phone call is by far more personal than any other medium and can go a long way in motivating a student. Some schools even require a phone call with each student at least once a month. That verbal interaction really cannot be replaced by any other form of communication and it's important to make it a priority in your daily work.

As a general rule, I try to make a phone call to a student when what I have to share with them is too complicated or too sensitive to be handled via e-mail or text messaging. If I find myself composing a two-paragraph e-mail and I'm nowhere close to done, it's best to just stop and place a phone call. That way I've not only answered a student's question but I've made a personal connection, which is well worth the time it took to dial the phone.

The only downside to making a phone call instead of communicating via another medium is that it's more difficult to keep accurate records of phone calls. Also, a student might think you said one thing when you thought you communicated a completely different message. Whenever a conversation is particularly controversial or touchy, you might want to consider recording it. That way there's a record for the future. Google Voice provides an option for recording incoming phone calls. You just have to press 4 during a conversation and it will be recorded and added to your voicemail in-box. There are also some other great options out there for recording those conversations at a moment's notice. At a minimum, every call should be logged with a brief summary of what was discussed. It helps not only teachers but also administrators to review all the details of a situation.

LMS Tools

In addition to e-mail, texting, IM, and phone calls, you'll also want to consider several tools in your LMS as a part of your methods of communication. Discussions, announcements, and grading feedback are all discussed in other areas of this text but don't forget that they can be powerful communication tools.

CHOOSING YOUR COMMUNICATION METHOD BASED ON MESSAGE

At this point we've examined a huge variety of communication tools and their uses. We know the power of communicating in different mediums for different students but it's also important to think about using different methods for different purposes. For particular issues, e-mails work best. For others, nothing will do but a phone call. As the teacher, it's important for you to make those distinctions well. Table 12.1 can help you decide which communication method you should use in a particular situation.

Table 12.1   Which Communication Tool Is Best?

Communication Tool	Best Uses
E-mail	Course reminders, important announcements, encouragement, answering student questions, notifying parents on course issues
Texting	Touching base with a nonengaged student, encouragement, brief interactions, procedural questions
IM	Just-in-time help with an assignment, explanations that are fairly straightforward, similar to texting but responses are generally quicker
Synchronous session	Any time that a screen share is necessary, technical troubleshooting, video conversations
Phone call	Multistep directions, discussing emotional issues, any time that tone of voice is important or questionable, resolving complex problems

Interview with Jane Good, Jeffco's 21st Century Virtual Academy

Jane Good is an online science teacher with Jeffco's 21st Century Virtual Academy in Golden, Colorado. Good teaches approximately 150 students each semester in grades 7–12 and says she really loves being able to reach her students in new ways.

Good says that before she became an online teacher, she had already figured out that the best way to teach kids is to be the facilitator of their learning instead of just a lecturer. However, online learning gave her the flexibility to truly customize for student's needs and focus on being a facilitator full-time. She tries to use a lot of front loading in her courses so that everything is clear from the beginning. She also spends a lot of time anticipating questions students might have and then clarifying that information in the course. However, Good says that often the most important thing she does in any given day is to work with students one-on-one.

Instead of thinking of all of her communication methods as separate from one another, Good views her communication options as a continuum of support. When a student falls behind or needs extra support, Good starts with an e-mail to that student. If that's unsuccessful, Good will call and talk the student through the problem. Then, if students still need further help or need something demonstrated visually, Good will move them into a webinar-style synchronous session. Through that webinar, Good can share her screen and visually demonstrate the concept. She says that using multiple streams of communication with the same student helps better meet the student's needs.

Good also is careful to make contact with struggling students as quickly as possible. She looks through her grade book at least every two weeks and makes a list of fifteen to twenty students who appear to be struggling, either because their grade has dropped or because Good hasn't heard from them recently. Then, she'll give all those students a personal phone call. Those phone calls might be a full day's worth of work but she says it's completely worth it to reach those students.

Overall, Good's best piece of advice to new online teachers is to make sure you keep the tone of your communications with students warm. She says to "come across as a human being. You use real language and humor so that it doesn't seem like reading a textbook. They should get a sense for who you are. Through that, students come to trust you and do better in your courses."

FOCUS ON BLENDED LEARNING

My experience with blended courses has shown me that, even though much of the classroom culture gets created in the face-to-face portion of the course, the relationships that I have with students still get developed primarily in the online portion of the course through digital communications, especially text messaging and e-mail. Students are very comfortable opening up in a digital format but tend to be more reserved with a larger audience inside our class time. It's important to still value those digital communications and initiate them on a regular basis as a part of the blended classroom routine. Digital communications also provide a timeliness to our feedback loop that simply wouldn't be possible if I waited until the next class meeting to have a face-to-face conversation. It's critical to use both methods to further relationships with students and provide them with the support they need.

CHAPTER THIRTEEN

TIME MANAGEMENT AND ROUTINES

ESSENTIAL QUESTIONS:

- How can I create a work-life balance when working from home?
- How is the work flow different in online learning than in a face-to-face class-room?
- What are some strategies for making my work more efficient?

MAKING THE TRANSITION

It was September of my first year of full-time online teaching. I had been working all day, only stopping to feed the kids and get them to bed. When my husband came in the front door after a night out, there I was typing away on my computer, still, at 10 P.M.! He rolled his eyes, closed my laptop, and said, "We need to talk. You started this job to have more time at home and with the family. Instead, you're always buried in the computer. Something has to give." He was right! It was at that moment I knew I had to find a new way to work. Just like with face-to-face teaching, there's always more to do when you're an online teacher. The workload can be crushing. Luckily, with a few changes in your routine, you can manage the workload far more effectively. In this chapter, we'll explore some of those strategies to make your time more efficient.

CREATING A WEEKLY ROUTINE

In a face-to-face classroom, much of your regular routine is governed by the bell schedule. Each day you move through answering e-mails, teaching first period, running to the restroom, grading a quick paper, teaching second period, planning for the next day, and so on. Somehow in that daily grind all the work of teaching eventually gets done (with some done at home!).

With online teaching, the rhythm is completely different. You'll find that instead of a daily routine for your work, governed by a bell schedule, you develop your own weekly routine. For example, every Monday you'll grade a particular class. On Tuesday, you might focus on creating course content. On Wednesday, you might focus on student phone calls. Developing that weekly routine can make a huge difference in your efficiency and in how effective you feel in your work. Instead of feeling like you need to tackle everything at once (as you did in a regular classroom!), you can just tackle the things on your to-do list for that day, knowing that the rest of the list is scheduled for other days in the upcoming week. Table 13.1 shows an example schedule assuming three preps, or different courses, that a teacher might be teaching. It can be modified for more preps as needed.

You can always add new items to your list as other things come up but your basic weekly to-do list provides a core structure to your week and helps you get things done efficiently.

TOP-THREE STRATEGY

Although a weekly to-do list and routines are a great first step, you'll still find that there are items on your to-do list that continually roll to the next day. Unfortunately there's sometimes just not enough time! One way to make sure that you're completing the most important things in each day is using a basic time management strategy called the *top three*. The premise is simple. When you create your to-do list for the day, either in the morning or the evening before, identify the items on your list that are your top three. These are the items that absolutely *have* to get done before your day is done. It could be that those items are time sensitive, they are essential to your workflow, or that you're simply tired of them being on the list! Then, when you begin to work on your to-do list for the day, those three items get first priority, above e-mails and above any other to-do items that may appear on your list. That way the most important things get done first and items that can wait may roll to the next list. You'll be amazed how quickly you can clear out a to-do list using this strategy!

Table 13.1 Sample Weekly Schedule

Monday	Tuesday	Wednesday	Thursday	Friday
Everyday tasks: Answer e-mails, text messages, and phone calls at least three times each day				
Grade class 1 Send struggling student e-mails Prep synchronous session for class 1 Send beginning-of-the-week e-mail	Grade class 2 Teach synchronous session for class 1 Send attendance e-mails	Grade class 3 Post weekly grades Prep synchronous sessions for classes 2 and 3 Make student phone calls for struggling students	Teach synchronous sessions for classes 2 and 3 Prep upcoming week course work for classes 1 and 2 Send way-to-go e-mails Text struggling students	Prep upcoming week course work for class 3 Send way-to-go e-mails Grade late work Send due date reminder e-mails

MANAGING THE E-MAIL MONSTER

One of the most challenging issues in time management for an online teacher is managing the e-mail monster. In any given day, you may receive up to 150 e-mails, all of which will need to be read, filed, and handled appropriately. If you allow it, e-mail will take over your workday and you may accomplish nothing else.

The first thing you'll need to do to manage the e-mail monster is to create an e-mail schedule. If you leave your e-mail program open and answer e-mails throughout the day, your work will be constantly interrupted by the lure of the e-mail ding. It's too easy to allow yourself to get distracted and off-task. For an online teacher, it's important to strike a balance between answering e-mails quickly and not allowing e-mail to become too large of a distraction. The best way to do that is to set two or three times during the day when you'll answer e-mails, usually in the morning, around noon, and toward the end of your work day. During those designated times, you'll completely clear out your in-box and deal with all emerging situations. However, the rest of the day, you'll leave e-mail closed and not allow it to distract you. Confining your e-mailing to those designated times will allow you to respond to e-mails in a timely manner and also provide some boundaries.

The second thing you'll want to do to manage the e-mail monster is to develop a filing system for e-mails. Most e-mail programs will allow you to create folders for sorting e-mails but labels or tags will work, too. For myself, I use four very basic folders.

First, I have a set of semester archive folders where I file any e-mails that have been taken care of. I can search the archive any time I need more information about a situation but the e-mails in that folder require no further action. Each semester I create a new archive folder for the new semester and all e-mails are filed there. That way I can quickly find e-mails about almost any situation from a particular semester.

Second, I have an encouragement folder. This is a folder for my own sanity. It contains e-mails from students, parents, or administrators that are particularly positive or encouraging. When I need a boost of motivation, I check here!

Third, I have a special projects folder. This folder is for ongoing projects such as a yearbook or course development in which the project is not complete and therefore can't be filed in the archive but I don't want those e-mails clogging up my in-box.

Finally, I have my basic in-box, where all e-mails are delivered. I include it in my list of essential folders because e-mails in my in-box have a specific purpose, too! Any e-mail that is left in my in-box requires action. At least once every few days, I review my in-box and try to take care of any lingering e-mails, those that I've read but haven't yet managed. My ultimate goal is to have a completely empty in-box by the end of my work day, totally ready for the student e-mails that will flood in overnight.

The final suggestion you'll want to follow to manage the e-mail monster is to turn off the e-mail notification on your phone and in your e-mail program. Although it can be nice to know you have a new e-mail, it can also become an obsession that interferes with your life! There's nothing worse than an e-mail ding at one in the morning. It wakes you up and keeps you from enjoying a good night's sleep. Because you know you'll be checking e-mail three times each day anyway, there's no reason to have further notification. You'll know you have e-mail when you check your account. There's no purpose for further stress.

These same rules can also be applied to text messages and other forms of communication. You want to be a quick communicator but it's also vital to put some boundaries on those forms of communication to make them more effective.

USING ADAPTIVE RELEASE

The next key for time management is to use adaptive release in your courses as much as possible. Adaptive release is a feature of your LMS that allows you to hide an item, folder, or announcement until a particular time in the future. This allows you to be present in your courses for your students even if you're not actually available. It also gives you the freedom to work ahead in a course. For example, if I need to remind students about an upcoming due date and I want that announcement to appear on a Friday, I can create the announcement on Tuesday with an adaptive release date of Friday. That way the announcement will appear for students on Friday, even if I happen to be in staff meetings all day. Students don't know the difference because it looks like I'm still actively posting in the course and adding announcements, even though I actually created them earlier in the week. That ability to consistently work ahead and hide things from students provides a huge benefit to your work day. You know that no matter what comes up the course is prepared for your students.

Adaptive release can also be a great way to keep your course clean and focused. Once a unit is done, don't be afraid to hide it from students and help them focus on the current work. If you haven't gotten to something yet, hide it! Students, like all of us, are easily distracted and the more clues you can give them about where to focus, the greater their odds of success.

CREATING A WORK-LIFE BALANCE

In order to prevent burnout in your online teaching life, you'll also want to explore some strategies for creating a positive work-life balance. Working from home can be difficult. One minute you're answering student e-mails, the next you're changing loads of laundry, and the next you're reviewing formative assessment data. It can be easy to let your work invade your life so much so that you never have time for your own personal life and leisure.

One of the easiest strategies for setting boundaries is to set working hours. You can let students know that you're available Monday through Friday from 8 A.M. to 6 P.M. (or another set of times that work for you and your students). Also let them know that outside of those hours, you won't be checking e-mails or returning phone calls. Those messages will get taken care of on the next work day but not during your down time. It's amazing how quickly students figure out to ask questions during usual working hours when they are answered within an hour or two. Not only that but they also come to respect your down time, too. They understand the need for family time and will respect your needs if you educate them early about when you're available and when you're not.

In my school, we've actually had to institute a "no e-mail on the weekends" policy for all of our teachers. There was a time when some teachers were answering e-mails on the weekend and others were not. Students became confused about expectations and wondered why some teachers didn't care enough to work all weekend! After we asked all teachers to refrain from answering e-mails on the weekend (or to use the "delay send" feature if they just couldn't help it), students started respecting the boundaries. The expectations were consistent across the board and, the truly amazing part, kids stopped e-mailing on the weekends! They realized it was best to wait and make contact on Monday. Those boundaries are vital and an important life lesson for all.

Once you have your work hours set, you'll want to take an additional step of actually turning off your computer when you're done working for the day or for the weekend. The lure of the glowing screen can be a powerful force. It entices you to do just one more thing until you find that you've worked all evening (trust me, I know!). Instead, try turning the computer completely off. The start-up process is usually too much of a pain for you to attempt any more work. You'll find you enjoy your evening more and can focus more on the important things—having some well-deserved leisure time!

This issue of time management is one that you'll continue to explore throughout your career. New tools, tips, and techniques will constantly evolve as your workload changes and your needs change, too. The beautiful thing is that online learning gives you that flexibility! Although not being tied to a bell schedule can be a foreign experience, it's also liberating! I hope you'll enjoy the journey as you learn to cope with new challenges.

Teacher Interview: Summer Reel, Guthrie Virtual School

Teacher Summer Reel, Spanish teacher for Guthrie Virtual School in Guthrie, Texas, knows all about the rigorous demands of being an online teacher. As a Spanish teacher in a rural area of Texas, she quickly found herself in high demand. Multiple districts needed a full-time Spanish teacher and there simply weren't enough bodies to fill all those classrooms! Instead of fighting over one teacher, Guthrie CSD decided to open an online Spanish course with Reel at the helm. At first, Reel simply paced her students through Rosetta Stone software, providing support as needed. Then, as Reel became more comfortable in the online environment, she began creating her own course and enriching the content. Now, three years later, she teaches two hundred students in any given semester in addition to being her school's registrar. Managing the workload can be a challenge!

Reel says that the adjustment her first year was difficult. The job isn't an 8-to-4 job like regular teaching and it can be hard to wrap your brain around that. Reel says she gets up really early to work on most mornings. She finds that 5:30–7:30 A.M. can be key working times because everyone else in the house is sleeping. It's quiet and you can accomplish a lot. She also says it's a great way to greet your students for the day. The first thing they'll see each morning is an encouraging message from their teacher! Then, she puts in short bursts of time throughout the day to get everything done that she needs to.

Reel also says that one of her challenges is finding a way to respond to kids in a timely way and not being glued to the iPhone all the time. She tries to find at least a few hours each day to be completely unplugged. Usually that time is from when her kids get home from school until they go to bed. That way she can completely focus on being together as a family.

Reel also says that clearing out the e-mail in-box right before bed is key to her sanity. "I like a tidy in-box at the end of the day so I can start my morning fresh."

Finally, what is Reel's advice to new online teachers? "You're going to be overwhelmed with all the communication and paper trail and documentation but one of the beauties of working in the online world is that you have those records. You have all that documentation. Just keep everything organized and it'll be fine!"

FOCUS ON BLENDED LEARNING

With a blended classroom format, the need for time management will be even more critical. In jumping from one format to another each day, it can be easy to feel torn in too many different directions. In managing your daily to-do list, it might be helpful to create two lists, one for items that are best done in the face-to-face environment and one for items that are best done in the quieter times when everyone is working online. Your face-to-face list might include items such as curriculum planning, calendar management, tutoring, and face-to-face student communications and your online list might include course building, assignment feedback, and digital communications. By splitting your list, you can avoid the temptation to do items that aren't very efficient when you're working in the wrong format. For example, it's not very efficient to text students during a face-to-face course so any texts received during that time will have to wait. Looking at it the other way, it's not very efficient to make a phone call to a student if you know you'll see that same student in a few hours in a face-to-face class period. By delineating the two workloads, you can make smarter decisions about managing tasks effectively.

CHAPTER FOURTEEN

STRATEGIES FOR BLENDED LEARNING

ESSENTIAL QUESTIONS:

- What is blended learning?
- How can I structure my face-to-face classroom to include blended learning?
- What assignments work well in a blended environment?
- How can I use online tools to make my work more efficient?

TOWARD A NEW WAY OF LEARNING

In recent years, *blended* (also called *hybrid*) learning has truly taken the education world by storm. What began as a small movement of online course options for face-to-face students has become an innovation that is invading traditional classrooms around the country. You'll find that most of the strategies in this book apply to both blended and fully online environments. However, the strategies in this chapter are meant to address the special challenges of working in a blended model, where some of the course is online and some is face-to-face.

BASIC BLENDED LEARNING MODELS

The first question we'll need to address is, "What is blended learning?" Blended learning, in its most basic form, is when a face-to-face classroom is blended with an online classroom to create the best of both worlds.

There are all sorts of models of blended learning and new ones are being created each year. Here are a few of the blended learning models identified by the Innosight Institute in *The Rise of K–12 Blended Learning* (Horn & Staker, 2011):

- *Face-to-face driver:* Course remains fully face-to-face but elements of the course are conducted online, such as online discussions, homework, or projects.

- *Rotation:* Students have some class time that is face-to-face and some class time that is fully online.

- *Flex:* The majority of the curriculum is provided online but teachers provide on-site support and tutoring.

- *Online lab:* A course is delivered fully online but it's done at a computer lab in a brick-and-mortar classroom. Teachers are usually provided online and a paraprofessional provides face-to-face support.

- *Self-blend:* Students choose which courses to take online and which to take in a brick-and-mortar classroom. Some of each school day is spent in both environments.

- *Online driver:* Courses and teachers are fully online with the teacher and student usually working remotely. These can be enriched by optional face-to-face activities.

It's sometimes helpful to think of these options on a continuum, on which class time is the greatest variable. On one side of the spectrum are courses that are still fully face-to-face with the course enriched by online options. On the other side of the spectrum are courses that are fully online but enriched by optional face-to-face activities. In most cases, a blended learning program will reside somewhere in the middle of the spectrum. Figure 14.1 helps demonstrate this concept.

If a course is living to the left of the spectrum, seat time is non-negotiable. The course meets for a traditional class period and a traditional amount of time. However, the grading and discussions might have moved mostly to an online course area and students are using that area regularly to access their course content. Or the teacher may have chosen to make the course paperless with all assignments

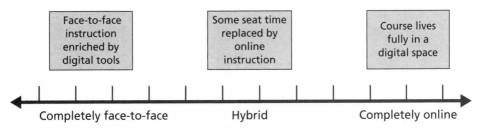

Figure 14.1 Continuum of Blended Learning Options

turned in to an online Dropbox. The varieties are endless but the core defining element of this side of the spectrum is that students are still in a regular classroom for a traditional amount of seat time.

If a course is living in the middle of the spectrum, some seat time has been replaced by online learning. Students might come to a course on Mondays and Wednesdays but during the rest of the work week they are working online exclusively. It might also be that students are in a face-to-face classroom Mondays through Thursdays with just Fridays online. Teachers in this model are constantly making the decision about which assignments lend themselves to online learning and which assignments should be done face-to-face. In many ways, students can have the best of both worlds in this option.

If a course is living to the right of the spectrum, the course is fully online with face-to-face time optional. In general, courses that are considered blended or hybrid will reside somewhere in the middle of this spectrum. However, in many cases, seat time is still non-negotiable. Students must be in the classroom for a regular class period for at least some of the time. Teachers in this situation shouldn't feel like they are stuck in a typical face-to-face model. Instead, they can create blended learning opportunities for their students by using an online space to organize their course and enrich it. It's amazing how much a course can be improved by simply using online tools on a regular basis.

LEARNING VARIABLES ON A DIGITAL SCALE

In the spectrum described here, seat time is the core variable in thinking about a blended course. However, there are quite a few more variables to consider. Sometimes you won't want to change seat time at all but instead put other elements online. What about assessment? Will students take all assessments in a face-to-face environment or can some of those move online? What about grading? Will students still turn in a piece of paper for each assignment or could some or all assignment

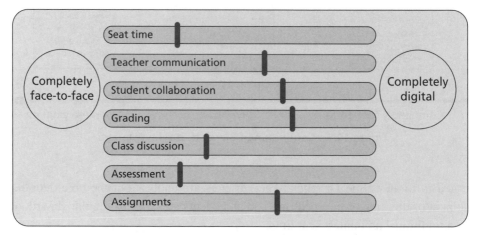

Figure 14.2 Class Variables on a Digital Spectrum

submissions be moved into an online space? How will that change or enrich the course? These variables and many others have to be considered as you think about how to create the best possible course for your students.

Figure 14.2 is a graphic of the different elements of a course that could be moved online. Think of it as a mixing board with sliders. As the teacher, you control the sliders and can make a decision about what parts of your course will reside where.

As you make decisions about how to create your blended course, there are several other choices to consider:

Personal preference: Think about which areas of the course you are most comfortable moving online. For example, a particular teacher could believe that class discussions are best done in a face-to-face environment because that best approximates the types of interactions students are likely to have when they enter the workplace. When this teacher builds her course, she won't focus on putting class discussions into the online space. Instead, maybe she'll be more comfortable putting some of her assignments online.

Tool availability: The kinds of tools you have available will go a long way toward dictating what you do online. For example, if your school has access to a tool that allows you to conduct great discussions online but doesn't really have a great grading tool, you may decide to focus on online discussions rather than online grading.

Course subject: Certain disciplines lend themselves better to online discussions than others. For example, a history teacher may be able to conduct some really robust discussions online. However, a math teacher might struggle. Therefore, the math teacher might focus more on creating online assignments and using the wealth of online videos that are available for math teachers, an area that history teachers may be lacking. You'll want to think about your content area and decide what to put online based on what works best for your needs. Remember that the purpose of blended learning is to use the best of both worlds. Make sure you're creating a course that uses the strengths of face-to-face learning and the strengths of online learning to create the best learning experience possible for your students.

EXAMPLE ACTIVITIES FOR A BLENDED ENVIRONMENT

A blended course has the bonus of creating both face-to-face and online experiences for students. Ideally, the course will include not just online and face-to-face components as separate elements but instead a series of blended assignments, in which a portion of the assignment takes place face-to-face and a portion of it is completed online. The best blended classrooms truly integrate the online portions of the course and the face-to-face portions to create a seamless whole. The following example assignments take advantage of the strengths of both formats:

- *Extending a discussion:* A teacher might prime the pump for a discussion by starting it out in the face-to-face environment. The teacher could introduce the topic and engage the students in a fifteen- to twenty-minute discussion. During that time, about 10 percent of the class will be able to contribute in a substantive way. Then, at the end of the period, the teacher can assign the rest of the discussion as homework. Students will then access the discussion via their home computer or a smartphone and expand on the ideas that were started in class. (See chapter 6 for more on discussion board strategies.)

- *Silent discussion:* Sometimes you might want all the students in your class to participate during a face-to-face discussion without the pressures of talking over each other or taking turns. One way to accomplish that is to begin the period with an online discussion. All the students contribute to the discussion board simultaneously in a face-to-face class. It's amazing how quiet a classroom can get when all the students are talking to each other in a virtual space! Then, once the discussion is wrapping up online, the students can summarize their learning in the face-to-face classroom, providing them with a written discussion as well as the opportunity to present their ideas in a physical space.

- *Collaborative website:* As a final project, groups of students can share their learning on a particular topic via a website. First, students collaborate together in their face-to-face classroom. They share the resources they're using and what content they'd like to use in their website. They also create the basic structure of their website when they're all there to share ideas. Then, using a tool such as Google Sites or Weebly, they can all go online and build their portion of the project. The result is a really in-depth website to demonstrate their understanding, created using face-to-face and online time.

- *Online assignment submission and grading:* A particular assignment can be explained and worked on in the face-to-face classroom when the teacher is there to answer initial questions and help students get started. Then, the assignment itself is submitted in an online space, either during the class period or later that night. The assignment is made in that face-to-face space but it's submitted and returned to students online, providing students with the opportunity to see immediate, in-depth feedback in the online space while also providing a time for Q&A in the physical classroom.

DESIGNING MIXED ASSIGNMENTS

The possibilities are really endless for creating assignments that mix elements of a face-to-face classroom with elements of an online classroom. The key is to use the strengths of each medium. Physical classrooms are best for real-time collaboration and verbal discussions whereas online classrooms excel for building collaborative projects, viewing video lectures, and participating in written discussions. Although either medium could work for any given task, it's important to think about which one works best for each task and then assign the work accordingly.

For example, let's say that you are a blended learning biology teacher who wants to have students study and do a series of presentations on various groups within the animal kingdom. If you were a fully online teacher, you might have students record their research in a wiki and then have them record their presentations in a screen-sharing program to upload to the online class. If you were a traditional teacher, you might have students do their research and share the presentations with the class. As a blended learning teacher, you can have the best of both worlds. Students could start out by recording all of their research in a wiki, collaborating together to find the best research information possible during the online portion of the class. Then, once the research is complete, students could share their presentations in the face-to-face portion of the course, giving them a live audience and live feedback. As a bonus, the presentations could even be recorded and uploaded to the online classroom for later viewing. The mixed assignment allows so much more to be possible than in a single format alone.

USING ONLINE TOOLS TO MAKE THE FACE-TO-FACE CLASSROOM MORE EFFICIENT

One of the most persuasive benefits of using the tools of a blended learning classroom to supplement the face-to-face classroom is that a teacher can be far more efficient. Instead of shuffling 150 papers for grading and entering, a teacher can simply have students submit their work online. The work can be graded and returned very quickly, with automatic entry into an online grade book. Instead of trying to keep track of discussion participation in the face-to-face classroom, an online discussion can be graded later and objectively evaluated for quantity and quality.

I'm often asked if I would ever return to a face-to-face classroom. My tentative answer is, ''Yes, if I had to, but the learning would look very different.'' I would at the very least use these online tools to create a more efficient classroom and, in the process, create a more in-depth learning experience for my students.

CHOOSING YOUR TOOLS

Sometimes one of the most overwhelming parts of moving to a blended learning model is simply the number of tools that are needed. It's difficult to imagine how you might manage all of your students' work online and also manage their use of all the tools they may need in that space.

Instead of thinking about using the entire Internet to supplement your blended course, it's best to think of your blended learning course in terms of a few basic tools. First, you'll need a home base for your students where they can find all the online elements of your course. That could be a blog, wiki, website, or a LMS such as Schoology, Edmodo, Blackboard, Moodle, and so on. I suggest using a LMS tool of some sort because it will come prebuilt with the discussion, grade book, content, and announcement tools that you'll need.

Second, you'll need to choose four to five tools that you want students to use on a regular basis. These are the core tools that students will use all the time and will become very familiar with. You'll probably want a wiki tool, a blog tool, a discussion space, and a grading tool. With those basic functions, you can create a really robust blended learning course. Many of them may be included in your LMS. At first, just focus on using those tools really well. Then, if you want to go deeper or use more complicated tools, you can experiment with them.

However, your core tools are already in place and those are the ones students will use regularly.

Moving into becoming a blended teacher can be really overwhelming. It's OK to start small. Before you know it, you'll have built a really robust online space that will adapt to meet the needs of multiple students. It's exciting work.

Interview with Brooke Fabian, East Boston High School

Teacher Brooke Fabian teaches English to a highly diverse population at East Boston High School in Massachusetts. This year, to meet the needs of a new bell schedule with less class time each day, Fabian started experimenting with blended learning. She says that she needed to find a way to maximize class time. Her solution was to move some of her content online and have students access that content from home.

At first, Fabian says she was concerned about making sure all students had access to the Internet at home or during the day away from her classroom. However, a quick poll of the class revealed that only three students in the entire class had no way to access the Internet at all. The others could all find ways via a friend's house, a smartphone, the library, or a home computer. After some troubleshooting with those three students, Fabian was able to ensure that her entire class had access. Then she jumped in to creating an online component for them. Fabian is careful to make sure that all assignments can be completed on a smartphone, an essential access point for a percentage of her class.

Now that Fabian has created an online portion to her course, she's finding that students are learning in ways that were never possible face-to-face. For example, students are creating blog entries in which they post vocabulary words. Then, other students find what they think are the best definitions for those words and share them in the comments. Fabian says she's amazed how many debates have happened in the comments section of her class blog over word usage. It's something that never happens face-to-face!

Fabian also says that her online discussions have begun to engage students that are only reluctant participators face-to-face. She says, "They will talk if I call on them but they never volunteer. In the online discussion, they post early and often. It's creating a new dynamic for their participation."

Although Fabian says that there can be hassles to using technology as an integral part of her course, she says, "The product is worth it." Students are creating things in her courses that "can't be created in any other venue." For example, freshmen who are finishing her course create Tumblr videos for incoming freshmen about how to succeed in high school. Amazingly, students are sharing their hearts in the videos, talking about how to excel, be yourself, and avoid bullying. Those kinds of products really make the blended course a rich learning environment!

CHAPTER FIFTEEN

TRAINING TO TEACH ONLINE

ESSENTIAL QUESTIONS:

- What is it like when you make the transition to being an online teacher?

- What options are available for training to teach online?

- What pitfalls can I expect in my first year of teaching online and how can I avoid them?

THE PROCESS OF BECOMING AN ONLINE TEACHER

The transition to becoming an online teacher can be difficult at times. In many ways, you're learning a whole new way of working and interacting with students. My first semester of teaching full-time online was a bit like being a student teacher all over again. I worked way too many hours and didn't know what I was doing far too much of the time! However, with training and experience, you'll quickly make a successful transition and feel far more comfortable in your new role.

All teachers will find that they have their own journey into teaching online. Some start as course developers, others jump right into teaching, and still others may get their feet wet by teaching just a single online course. Personally, I started as a course developer. Looking back, it's clear that I had no business developing an online course before I had actually taught one but it was a great first step in learning the tools I needed to teach well online. In this chapter, I'll share a continuum of ways to get started in teaching online. Although I think that it's best to start with the first items listed in this chapter (taking an online course) and move gradually into the last items listed (being an administrator), every teacher will find his or her own path along the way.

TAKING AN ONLINE COURSE

One of the best things you can do when you first become interested in online teaching is to take an online course in your subject area or an area of interest. Local community college courses, which are increasingly taught online, are great, inexpensive options for finding out what online learning is all about by becoming a student. There's no substitute for becoming an online student and dealing with all the joys and challenges that your students will face in your classroom.

During that student experience, you'll want to pay careful attention to your professor and look for a few key elements:

- How does the professor make him- or herself present in the online course?

- What role is the professor playing in classroom discussions?

- How is the professor using announcements to connect with the course?

- What kinds of feedback are you getting in your online assignments? Is that feedback helpful?

- Do you feel like you've gotten to know your professor and his or her expectations? Why or why not?

- Do you interact with other classmates? How did those relationships develop?

Even if you find yourself in an online course with a bad online teacher, this can be a learning experience. In watching what doesn't work in an online course, you'll learn just as much (if not more!) about the kind of online teacher you want to be.

ONLINE TRAINING COURSES AND PROFESSIONAL DEVELOPMENT BOOKS

Once you've taken an online course and have a good understanding of the student experience in an online class, your next step should be to seek out further training about how to teach online. One option to consider is an online teacher certification program. Many state universities are developing programs to train existing teachers in the nuances of how to teach online. Usually these certificate programs include three to four courses for twelve to fifteen credit hours. Another bonus is that most of these programs are taught online, providing even more experience in what a good online course looks like. Currently Boise State University has one of the leading programs in the country for online learning. You should also be able to find a local program. Although this type of preparation is an investment, it can also give you a great edge when you're competing for your first online teaching job.

Another option to consider is taking an online course on how to be an online teacher. PBS Teacherline (www.pbs.org/teacherline) has an excellent one titled "Online Facilitation Strategies I." This was the course that I took when I first seriously considered teaching online. It was the first time I really considered what my philosophy of online teaching might look like. By the end of the course, I felt I had a really robust understanding of the kind of online teacher I wanted to be and what strategies I needed to use to get there. Ed Tech Leaders Online (http://edtechleaders.org) also has a basic training course that is worth considering.

Finally, you'll want to continue reading everything you can about online learning and online teaching strategies. Reading this book is a great start! You'll also want to review the iNACOL National Standards for Quality Online Teaching. They can be a great way to assess your own skills and think about where you'd like to grow in the coming semesters. (See appendix C for a complete copy of the standards.).

Jossey-Bass has also published a series of books about online teaching. Some of the titles include *Engaging the Online Learner, Managing Online Instructor Workload*, and *Assessing the Online Learner*. Although the texts are primarily written for college-level teachers, the strategies can easily be adapted to use with middle school and high school students. As your skills progress, you'll find these books to be a great resource for growing deeper.

TEACHING PART-TIME ONLINE

Once you've completed some basic training for teaching online and become an online student yourself, you'll be ready to start actually teaching in an online classroom. I suggest teaching part-time online before you move into a full-time position. This type of teaching is not for everyone and teaching part-time first can help you decide if online teaching is something you want to continue to pursue. Thankfully there are lots of options for part-time teaching positions; you can moonlight online while still teaching in a regular classroom. Your state virtual school is a great place to start your search.

TAKING ON MORE ADVANCED ROLES

If you've moved through all these roles—being an online student, taking an online teacher training course, and teaching part-time online—then you'll be well prepared to take on any new roles in online learning that come your way. Some of those may include teaching full-time online, developing online courses, or being an administrator for an online program. Although it is possible to take on these more advanced roles without all the preparation I've listed here, it will be extremely difficult. Online learning is a completely different way of teaching and learning and it can take a while to make the adjustment.

WHAT TO EXPECT DURING THE TRANSITION

The transition to part-time or full-time online teaching will be overwhelming at first, regardless of what kind of preparation you've put in ahead of time. The bottom line is that your job has changed drastically. Give yourself some freedom to experiment and even make mistakes. It's OK to feel like a student teacher again. In some ways, you will be a student teacher and that's completely normal.

During your first semester of teaching online, be prepared for a very different feel for your work life. Instead of a day clearly defined by bell schedules and arriving students, your work life will seep into your entire day, sometimes meaning that you're up answering e-mails at 5 A.M. or still answering text messages at 10 P.M. The e-mails, phone calls, text messages, and so on may seem like they never stop. This is especially true of the first few weeks when students are getting oriented to your class and finding out how everything works. You may find yourself wanting to throw the computer across the room and give it all up! Instead, please take a deep breath and slow down. Realize that this is a huge adjustment and give yourself some room to grow. Put in place some parameters so that you still have a personal life in addition to your online courses. Read (or reread) chapter 13 on time management and make some adjustments. You'll soon find new ways to work and won't be able to imagine doing your work any other way!

FINDING A MENTOR OR MENTOR COMMUNITY

During your first semester as an online teacher, you'll also want to make the time to develop a mentor relationship with another online teacher in your program (or in another program if you're on your own). Whether this is a formal mentorship set up by your school or an informal one created from necessity, having another teacher you can go to for help is essential! From simple technology questions to lofty questions about teaching philosophy, having another sympathetic ear is vital. If possible, try to make sure that mentor has taught online for at least two years and preferably with the age group that you're working with. Then, politely ask if you can occasionally call on him or her for help. It pays to be humble! Most teachers are more than willing to help. It can even be a good idea to set up a monthly phone call or coffee date so you can just debrief together. You'll be amazed how many questions you may have and how much you'll challenge each other's learning!

AVOIDING ISOLATION AND CONNECTING WITH OTHER ONLINE TEACHERS

In addition to finding a mentor, you'll also want to be purposeful about creating relationships with other online teachers. In most teaching situations, you'll proba-bly work from home with limited contact with your colleagues. In the absence of a water cooler, it's important to create some other options for sharing ideas and venting frustrations.

One of the best ways to create some just-in-time connections with your colleagues is to use a schoolwide IM system. At my school we use Google Chat but Windows Messenger and Skype are also great options. Any time a teacher is working at his or her computer and available to talk, he or she should be signed in to the IM program. Then, if someone has a quick troubleshooting question or a question about a student, the teacher can just glance at the IM program and find someone to help. It gives online teachers that just-down-the-hall feeling that you used to have in a regular building.

In addition to IM, it's also helpful to cultivate some ''water cooler buddy'' relationships. These are the teachers in your program whom you trust to be there with advice or just a friendly ear. When you find yourself frustrated or confused about something, you can give that teacher a call and ask anything, even really dumb questions. You can also share your frustrations with that person, knowing that he or she will keep them in confidence. Sometimes you just need to share an idea with someone and vice versa. Knowing that you have someone just a phone call, e-mail, or IM away is incredibly reassuring.

Just like face-to-face teaching, becoming an online teacher can be a long process of trial and error. In this book you'll find some basic strategies for how to teach well in this new environment but ultimately there is no substitute for actually doing the work. The really great part? The process can be a lot of fun!

Interview with Hannah Brown, ECOT, Columbus, Ohio

Hannah Brown just finished her first year as an online art teacher for ECOT, the Electronic Classroom of Tomorrow School, based in Columbus, Ohio. Each semester, she worked with approximately 220 students in a beginning art course, teaching everything from shading to linear perspective. Hannah says that her first year has been a challenge but it's also been incredibly rewarding.

During the first year, Brown says she's made some significant adjustments in the way she teaches. For example, she quickly realized that she couldn't teach students about linear perspective without physically showing them what it looks like and how to create it on paper. Students just weren't getting it any other way. So, she implemented a video series in which she demonstrates a concept to students and shares that in the online course environment. Then students can watch the video as they create their assignments.

Although Brown did have some early professional development about how to teach online, her most helpful resource was a great mentor. Brown says she called her mentor all year with all sorts of questions, not only tech questions but also student motivation and relationship questions. Having that formal mentor relationship really sped up her learning process. Instead of having to seek out a mentor or feel embarrassed about asking questions of other teachers, she knew from day one whom to call and that the person on the other end of the line would always be helpful. As a result, Brown says she never panicked and just asked questions any time she needed help.

Brown says that overall she finds online teaching incredibly rewarding. Each semester she "sees kids move from dropping out to straight A students" and that makes it all worthwhile!

FOCUS ON BLENDED LEARNING

Most of the strategies mentioned in this chapter will also apply to preparing to become a blended learning teacher. Because blended learning combines face-to-face instruction with online instruction, you'll want to make sure you have some experience with both paradigms (as a student or a teacher) before heading into a blended learning classroom. More and more universities are offering blended courses and taking one of those courses can be a great way to get your feet wet and gain a basic understanding of what's possible in a blended classroom.

In addition, blended learning teachers often have the benefit of deciding how much of their course they want to blend. If you're anxious about adding online elements to your traditional course, it's OK to start small. Simply adding some online components such as discussions or Dropboxes is a great way to start.

iNACOL NATIONAL STANDARDS FOR QUALITY ONLINE COURSES

SECTION A: CONTENT

Description: The course provides online learners with multiple ways of engaging with learning experiences that promote their mastery of content and are aligned with state or national content standards.

Academic Content Standards and Assessments

1. The goals and objectives clearly state what the participants will know or be able to do at the end of the course. The goals and objectives are measurable in multiple ways.

2. The course content and assignments are aligned with the state's content standards, common core curriculum, or other accepted content standards set for Advanced Placement courses, technology, computer science, or other courses whose content is not included in the state standards.

Note: The iNACOL National Standards for Quality Online Courses are reprinted with permission from iNACOL (2011). All rights reserved.

3. The course content and assignments are of sufficient rigor, depth, and breadth to teach the standards being addressed.

4. Information literacy and communication skills are incorporated and taught as an integral part of the curriculum.

5. Multiple learning resources and materials to increase student success are available to students before the course begins.

Course Overview and Introduction

6. A clear, complete course overview and syllabus are included in the course.

7. Course requirements are consistent with course goals, are representative of the scope of the course, and are clearly stated.

8. Information is provided to students, parents, and mentors on how to communicate with the online instructor and course provider.

Legal and Acceptable Use Policies

9. The course reflects multicultural education, and the content is accurate, current, and free of bias or advertising.

10. Expectations for academic integrity, use of copyrighted materials, plagiarism and netiquette (Internet etiquette) regarding lesson activities, discussions, and e-mail communications are clearly stated.

11. Privacy policies are clearly stated.

Instructor Resources

12. Online instructor resources and notes are included.

13. Assessment and assignment answers and explanations are included.

SECTION B: INSTRUCTIONAL DESIGN

Description: The course uses learning activities that engage students in active learning and provides students with multiple learning paths to master; the content is based on student needs and provides ample opportunities for interaction and communication—student to student, student to instructor, and instructor to student.

Instructional and Audience Analysis

1. Course design reflects a clear understanding of all students' needs and incorporates varied ways to learn and master the curriculum.

Course, Unit, and Lesson Design

2. The course is organized by units and lessons that fall into a logical sequence. Each unit and lesson includes an overview describing objectives, activities, assignments, assessments, and resources to provide multiple learning opportunities for students to master the content.

Instructional Strategies and Activities

3. The course instruction includes activities that engage students in active learning.

4. The course and course instructor provide students with multiple learning paths, based on student needs, that engage students in a variety of ways.

5. The course provides opportunities for students to engage in higher-order thinking, critical reasoning activities, and thinking in increasingly complex ways.

6. The course provides options for the instructor to adapt learning activities to accommodate students' needs.

7. Readability levels, written language assignments, and mathematical requirements are appropriate for the course content and grade-level expectations.

Communication and Interaction

8. The course design provides opportunities for appropriate instructor-student interaction, including opportunities for timely and frequent feedback about student progress.

9. The course design includes explicit communication and activities (before and during the first week of the course) that confirms whether students are engaged and are progressing through the course. The instructor will follow program guidelines to address nonresponsive students.

10. The course provides opportunities for appropriate instructor-student and student-student interaction to foster mastery and application of the material.

Resources and Materials

11. Students have access to resources that enrich the course content.

SECTION C: STUDENT ASSESSMENT

Description: The course uses multiple strategies and activities to assess student readiness for and progress in course content and provides students with feedback on their progress.

Evaluation Strategies

1. Student evaluation strategies are consistent with course goals and objectives, are representative of the scope of the course, and are clearly stated.

2. The course structure includes adequate and appropriate methods and procedures to assess students' mastery of content.

Feedback

3. Ongoing, varied, and frequent assessments are conducted throughout the course to inform instruction.

4. Assessment strategies and tools make the student continually aware of his or her progress in class and mastery of the content.

Assessment Resources and Materials

5. Assessment materials provide the instructor with the flexibility to assess students in a variety of ways.

6. Grading rubrics are provided to the instructor and may be shared with students.

7. The grading policy and practices are easy to understand.

SECTION D: TECHNOLOGY

Description: The course takes full advantage of a variety of technology tools, has a user-friendly interface, and meets accessibility standards for interoperability and access for learners with special needs.

Course Architecture

1. The course architecture permits the online instructor to add content, activities, and assessments to extend learning opportunities.

2. The course accommodates multiple school calendars, for example, block, 4X4, and traditional schedules.

User Interface

3. Clear and consistent navigation is present throughout the course.

4. Rich media are provided in multiple formats for ease of use and access in order to address diverse student needs.

Technology Requirements and Interoperability

5. All technology requirements (including hardware, browser, software, and so on) are specified.

6. Prerequisite skills in the use of technology are identified.

7. The course uses content-specific tools and software appropriately.

8. The course is designed to meet internationally recognized interoperability standards.

9. Copyright and licensing status, including permission to share when applicable, is clearly stated and easily found.

Accessibility

10. Course materials and activities are designed to provide appropriate access to all students. The course, developed with universal design principles in mind, conforms to the US Section 504 and Section 508 provisions for electronic and information technology as well as the W3C's Web Content Accessibility guidelines (WCAg 2.0).

Data Security

11. Student information remains confidential, as required by the Family Educational Rights and Privacy Act (FERPA).

SECTION E: COURSE EVALUATION AND SUPPORT

Description: The course is evaluated regularly for effectiveness, using a variety of assessment strategies, and the findings are used as a basis for improvement. The course is kept up to date, both in content and in the application of new research on course design and technologies. Online instructors and their students are prepared to teach and learn in an online environment and are provided support during the course.

Assessing Course Effectiveness

1. The course provider uses multiple ways of assessing course effectiveness.

2. The course is evaluated using a continual improvement cycle for effectiveness and the findings are used as a basis for improvement.

Course Updates

3. The course is updated periodically to ensure that the content is current.

Certification

4. Course instructors, whether face-to-face or virtual, are certificated and "highly qualified." The online course teacher possesses a teaching credential from a state-licensing agency and is "highly qualified" as defined under ESEA (Elementary and Secondary Education Act).

Instructor and Student Support

5. Professional development about the online course delivery system is offered by the provider to ensure effective use of the courseware and various instructional media available.

6. The course provider offers technical support and course management assistance to students, the course instructor, and the school coordinator.

7. Course instructors, whether face to-face or virtual, have been provided professional development in the behavioral, social, and, when necessary, emotional aspects of the learning environment.

8. Course instructors, whether face-to-face or virtual, receive instructor professional development, which includes the support and use of a variety of communication modes to stimulate student engagement online.

9. The provider ensures that course instructors, whether face-to-face or virtual, are provided support, as needed, to ensure their effectiveness and success in meeting the needs of online students.

10. Students are offered an orientation for taking an online course before starting the course work.

SAMPLE SYLLABUS

English 12 Syllabus

Spring 2012

Kristin Kipp

Welcome to English 12B. I'm so glad to have you as a part of our class. Please read this information carefully because it will give you a clear understanding of the expectations for my class.

Course Overview

English 12B is a study of literature. We'll tackle everything from nonfiction to science fiction with several goat trails in between! You can expect your reading, writing, and thinking skills to be challenged throughout. Take a look at the chart below for an overview of the whole course.

#	Unit Title	Content	Approximate Length and Semester	Approximate Month
5	Drama part 2: *The Importance of Being Earnest* (after break)	Wilde's *The Importance of Being Earnest*	3 weeks, spring semester	Jan.

(continued)

(continued)

#	Unit Title	Content	Approximate Length and Semester	Approximate Month
6	English poets	Overview study of the major British poets	5 weeks, spring semester	Feb.–Mar.
7	Novel study: science fiction	Choose one novel from the sci-fi option list	5 weeks, spring semester	Mar.–Apr.
8	Short story	Short story study	3 weeks, spring semester	Apr.–May
9	Review and final	Final exam	1 week, spring semester	May

Materials Needed

Most of the texts we will read in class will be available online. However, you will need to find copies of the following texts. They should be readily available at the public library, a bookstore, or a used bookstore.

Second Semester Required Texts

Pick *one* of these (for the sci-fi unit). We'll start this unit in March so you have until then to borrow or purchase one of these texts:

- *Anthem* by Ayn Rand

- *1984* by George Orwell

- *20,000 Leagues under the Sea* by Jules Verne

- *Brave New World* by Aldous Huxley

- *Fahrenheit 451* by Ray Bradbury

    I strongly suggest that you choose one of the novels that you have not read before because it will make the unit far more meaningful for you.

Optional Texts (Because There Are Versions Available Online and, in Some Cases, We May Only Read Excerpts)

- *The Importance of Being Earnest* by Oscar Wilde

- *Beowulf*

- *Canterbury Tales* by Geoffrey Chaucer

  All other readings will be provided online.

Other Office Supplies That May Be Helpful

- A notebook or folder to store paper copies of texts that you print out

- Pen and pencil

- Highlighter

- Printer and printer paper

Software

- A basic Office suite of software (a word processor and presentation software). If you do not have Microsoft Office on your computer, you might consider downloading Open Office. It's a free suite of Office software that functions very much like Microsoft Office.

- A web browser. I prefer that you have two options because sometimes a particular tool won't work on one browser but will on another. I use Firefox and Internet Explorer. Both are available free online.

- Windows Messenger. This is an instant messenger program that is available free. I am on IM most of the day on weekdays. It's a great way to get quick questions answered. My IM address is the same as my e-mail address.

- A functional e-mail address <u>that you check every day</u>. I expect to be able to contact you within twenty-four hours on your e-mail address.

Course Expectations

This online course is the equivalent of a face-to-face English course. As such, there are basic expectations that every student should expect to follow.

Time

Each **Wednesday** morning you will receive one week's worth of assignments. For the average student they should take five to seven hours to complete. That time should be spread out over the week with a little each weekday. That week's assignments will be due the following **Tuesday** before midnight. I strongly suggest using the week's "Suggested Schedule" (found in the announcements) to help you stay on track.

Due Dates

All due dates can be found under the "Calendar/Due Dates" button in the course as well as in the "Course Announcements." **In general, you can expect your weekly assignments to be due Tuesday before midnight.**

Office Hours

I host virtual office hours a couple of times a week. They are a great time to come by and get help or ask questions. You can find the link to attend office hours by clicking on the "Attend Live" button in our class and then clicking on "Ms. Kipp's Classroom and Office Hours" and "Enter."

Check the Google Calendar under the "Calendar/Due Dates" button to find out when the next office hours will be.

Live Class Sessions (Virtual Classes in a Webinar on Your Browser)

There will be one live class session each week. The usual time for live sessions in this course is **Wednesday at 4:30 P.M.** Live sessions are a great time for questions and discussions. They generally last twenty to forty minutes. It's important that you make them a priority.

Live sessions are optional for class but they can be a great way to get your questions answered. If you are unable to attend the live sessions, you may watch the recording at any time.

You can attend a live session by clicking on the "Attend Live" button in our course and then clicking on "Ms. Kipp's Classroom and Office Hours."

Late-Work Policy

Just as in a face-to-face classroom, it is important that you complete your work in a timely fashion. **Late assignments may be turned in within the current unit only and can earn up to 75 percent credit.** After that there is no late credit available.

Example: During Unit 3 you may turn in any late assignments from Unit 3 for up to 75 percent credit but once we start Unit 4, Unit 3 is closed and no late work will be taken.

The last day for late work will be posted on the Google Calendar for each unit. It's usually about seven days after the last due date for that unit. Check under the "Calendar/Due Dates" button and in "Course Announcements" to keep up-to-date on your course work!

This late-work policy does *not* apply to discussion board postings. There is no late credit available for discussion boards because the rest of the class will have already moved on. Participating late in a discussion is like walking into a classroom late and talking to yourself about the content. No one is there to hear you and it doesn't benefit the class!

If you have an emergency or extenuating circumstance and you know you will not be able to get your assignments in on time, contact me individually for an extension. I am usually willing to work with you.

Attendance

The state requires us to enter attendance each day. Therefore you must log in every school day, Monday through Friday. Sometimes you may log in just to check announcements and the discussion boards. Other times you may work for a longer period of time. How you allocate your work time (five to seven hours per week) is up to you but you must log in each weekday so I can count you "present" for that day.

I take attendance each day around 3 P.M. and I count attendance for the previous twenty-four hours. If you log in after that time, that log-in will be counted for the next day's attendance. On Monday's I count log-ins from Friday at 3 P.M. until Monday at 3 P.M. as Monday's attendance. Please let me know if you have questions about attendance or a special situation.

Here are some examples that may help:

Log-in Day and Time	Counts as Attendance on
Tuesday at 2:00 P.M.	Tuesday
Tuesday at 3:30 P.M.	Wednesday
Friday at 5:00 P.M.	Monday

Discussion Boards

The discussion boards are a vital part of our classroom community and are worth a significant portion of your final grade. Please visit them regularly and actively participate.

There is a space for socializing in the forum. Please keep your discussions school appropriate.

There is also a troubleshooting space in the forum. If you are having a problem that could affect other members of the class, post here first rather than e-mailing. Your question will probably get answered more quickly here and, if other students have the same question, they can refer to your answer. *Students who regularly assist other students in the troubleshooting area will receive extra credit at the end of the semester.*

Plagiarism

Be very careful to avoid plagiarism. All plagiarized assignments will receive a zero and could have further disciplinary actions. When in doubt, cite the work or don't use it! Ask me if you need assistance on citing sources or paraphrasing.

Netiquette

What is netiquette? The word itself is a combination of the words *Internet* and *etiquette*. Netiquette is a set of expectations, sometimes stated and sometimes not, for how people interact in cyberspace. Always remember that you are talking to a real person. Respect that above all else and we shouldn't have any problems in this course.

Here are some other rules to remember:

- Avoid talking in all caps. It means that you're shouting at someone!

- The tone of your message is really important. If you think it might not be clear that you're joking, use an emoticon so no one gets offended.:)

- Keep your messages to the point. If there's a lot of scrolling, people probably won't read and respond to your thoughts. We want to keep the discussion going but we don't want to turn people off with long diatribes.

- Never write anything in the course that you wouldn't be comfortable with printing in your local newspaper to be read by all your friends and family.

- If you get upset by a message, take a little break. Don't respond when you're angry. Take a little while to think about it first!

- Always be polite. Remember, you're dealing with real people, not just words on a screen.

Getting Help

One of the most important things you can do as an online learner is know when to ask for help. Unlike in a classroom, I can't see your face to know when you're confused or frustrated. **It's very important that you communicate with me and let me know what you need!**

It is important to remember that technology cannot be used as an excuse for not turning in assignments. Think of technology as your car. If your car broke down in a traditional school, would you stop attending class? It doesn't work in an online school either. Always find another way to get your work done!

The following chart gives you an idea of what kinds of problems you might run into and whom you can contact for help.

Problem	Steps to Take
Don't understand the directions on an assignment	• Post to troubleshooting discussion board • Attend office hours • E-mail Ms. Kipp
Trouble submitting an assignment	• Post to troubleshooting discussion board • E-mail Ms. Kipp
Problems with Blackboard	• Clear your Internet cache and temporary files • Refer to Blackboard technical manual from J21VA • Call help desk • E-mail Ms. Kipp
Problem with a grade or needing an extension	• E-mail Ms. Kipp
Problems with your personal computer	• Restart your computer • Clear your Internet cache and temporary files • Contact your service provider or parent • E-mail Ms. Kipp to let her know the problem and when it will be solved

(continued)

(continued)

Problem	Steps to Take
Problems with a file type not going into Blackboard	• Refer to the supported file types for Blackboard • Post to the discussion board • For documents, try saving them as .rtf
Problems with Internet connection	• Contact your service provider • Work at a friend's house or the local library until the problem is resolved (so you don't fall behind)

Assessment

Letter grades will be assigned according to a standard distribution with rounding:

89.5%–100% A

79.5%–89.4% B

69.5%–79.4% C

59.5%–69.4% D

<59.5% F

I strongly suggest that you check "My Grades" on a regular basis to make sure that your grade is where you want it to be.

You'll also want to regularly check graded assignments and **read comments**. I give in-depth feedback on every assignment so you know how to improve.

If you ever think there is a problem with a grade, please call or e-mail me. I'm happy to discuss it.

Again, welcome to class. Please contact me if you have any questions!

Ms. Kipp

iNACOL NATIONAL STANDARDS FOR QUALITY ONLINE TEACHING

Standard A: The online teacher knows the primary concepts and structures of effective online instruction and is able to create learning experiences to enable student success.

Teacher Knowledge and Understanding	Teacher Abilities
The online teacher knows and understands the current best practices and strategies for online teaching and learning and their implementation in online education.	The online teacher is able to apply the current best practices and strategies in online teaching to create rich and meaningful experiences for students.

(continued)

(continued)

Teacher Knowledge and Understanding	Teacher Abilities
The online teacher knows and understands the role of online learning in preparing students for the global community they live in, both now and in the future.	The online teacher is able to build learner capacity for collaboration in face-to-face, blended, and online environments and encourages students to participate as global citizens.
The online teacher knows and understands the instructional delivery continuum (for example, fully online to blended to face-to-face).	[This indicator can only be evaluated in the context of instructor(s) having the ability to modify the course.] The online teacher is able to construct flexible, digital, and interactive learning experiences that are useful in a variety of delivery modes.
The online teacher knows and understands the need for continuing to update academic knowledge, pedagogy, and skills.	The online teacher is able to meet the state's professional teaching standards or has academic credentials in the field in which he or she is teaching.
The online teacher knows and understands the subject area and age group they are teaching.	The online teacher is able to provide evidence of credentials in the field of study to be taught.
The online teacher knows and understands the professional responsibility to contribute to the effectiveness, vitality, and self-renewal of the teaching profession, as well as to their online school and community.	

Standard B: The online teacher understands and is able to use a range of technologies, both existing and emerging, that effectively support student learning and engagement in the online environment.

Teacher Knowledge and Understanding	Teacher Abilities
The online teacher knows and understands the use of an array of grade-appropriate online tools for communication, productivity, collaboration, analysis, presentation, research, and content delivery.	The online teacher is able to select and use a variety of online tools for communication, productivity, collaboration, analysis, presentation, research, and online content delivery as appropriate to the content area and student needs.
The online teacher knows and understands the use of emerging technologies in a variety of mediums for teaching and learning, based on student needs.	The online teacher is able to effectively use and incorporate subject-specific and developmentally appropriate technologies, tools, and resources.
The online teacher knows and understands the importance of interaction in an online course and the role of varied communication tools in supporting interaction.	The online teacher is able to use communication technologies in a variety of mediums and contexts for teaching and learning.
The online teacher knows and understands basic troubleshooting skills and the responsibility to address basic technical issues online students may have.	The online teacher is able to apply troubleshooting skills (for example, change passwords, download plug-ins, and so on).
The online teacher knows and understands the need to continuously update their knowledge and skills for using the evolving technology tools that support online learning.	The online teacher is able to identify and explore new tools and test their applicability to their content areas and students.

Standard C: The online teacher plans, designs, and incorporates strategies to encourage active learning, application, interaction, participation, and collaboration in the online environment.

Teacher Knowledge and and Understanding	Teacher Abilities
The online teacher knows and understands the techniques and applications of online instructional strategies, based on current research and practice (for example, discussion, student-directed learning, collaborative learning, lecture, project-based learning, forum, small group work).	The online teacher is able to use student-centered instructional strategies that are connected to real-world applications to engage students in learning (for example, peer-based learning, inquiry-based activities, collaborative learning, discussion groups, self-directed learning, case studies, small group work, and guided design).
The online teacher knows and understands the process for facilitating, monitoring, and establishing expectations for appropriate interaction among students.	The online teacher is able to facilitate and monitor appropriate interaction among students.
The online teacher knows and understands the techniques for developing a community among the participants.	The online teacher is able to apply effective facilitation skills by creating a relationship of trust; establish consistent and reliable expectations; and support and encourage independence and creativity that promotes the development of a sense of community among the participants.
The online teacher knows and understands the process for facilitating and monitoring online instruction groups that are goal-oriented, focused, project-based, and inquiry-oriented to promote learning through group interaction.	The online teacher is able to facilitate and monitor online instruction groups to promote learning through higher-order thinking and group interaction.

Teacher Knowledge and and Understanding	Teacher Abilities
The online teacher knows and understands techniques to adjust communications to diverse perspectives.	The online teacher is able to respond appropriately to the diverse backgrounds and learning needs of the students.
The online teacher knows and understands differentiated instruction based on students' learning styles.	The online teacher is able to use differentiated strategies in conveying ideas and information, and is able to assist students in assimilating information to gain understanding and knowledge.
The online teacher knows and understands techniques to create an environment that will engage, welcome, and reach each individual learner.	The online teacher is able to apply strategies for engagement in online learning environments (for example, asking questions to stimulate discussion).
The online teacher knows and understands participation in an online course from a student-centered approach.	The online teacher is able to apply experiences as an online student and/or group to demonstrate the development and implementation of successful strategies for online teaching environments and to anticipate challenges and problems in the online classroom.
The online teacher knows and understands the need to establish and maintain ongoing and frequent teacher-student interaction, student-student interaction, teacher-parent interaction, and teacher-mentor interaction.	The online teacher is able to provide a variety of ongoing and frequent teacher-student interaction, student-student interaction, teacher-parent interaction, and teacher-mentor interaction opportunities.

Standard D: The online teacher promotes student success through clear expectations, prompt responses, and regular feedback.

Teacher Knowledge and Understanding	Teacher Abilities
The online teacher knows and understands techniques to maintain strong and regular communication with students, using a variety of tools.	The online teacher is able to use effective communication skills with students.
The online teacher knows and understands techniques for using appropriate communications in support of student engagement through prompt and regular feedback, and setting and communicating high expectations.	The online teacher is able to provide prompt feedback, communicate high expectations, and respect diverse talents and learning styles.
The online teacher knows and understands the need to create and explain objectives, concepts, and learning outcomes in a clearly written, concise format and to explain the course organization to students.	The online teacher is able to provide clear definitions of objectives, concepts, and learning outcomes and the course organization to students.
The online teacher knows and understands the need to define the terms of class interaction for both teacher and students.	The online teacher is able to establish and provide clear expectations of class interaction for both teacher and students.
The online teacher knows and understands the need to define the assessment criteria for the course.	The online teacher is able to provide a clear explanation of the assessment criteria for the course to students.
The online teacher knows and understands the need to provide clear expectations for teacher response time to student queries.	The online teacher is able to provide a clear explanation of the expectations of teacher response time to student queries.

Teacher Knowledge and Understanding	Teacher Abilities
The online teacher knows and understands the need to establish criteria for appropriate online behavior for both teacher and students.	The online teacher is able to establish and implement criteria for appropriate online behavior for both teacher and students.
The online teacher knows and understands the need for timely, constructive, personalized feedback to students about assignments and questions.	The online teacher is able to use student data to inform instruction, guide and monitor students' management of their time, monitor learner progress with available tools, and develop an intervention plan for unsuccessful learners.
The online teacher knows and understands a variety of methods and tools to reach and engage students who are struggling.	The online teacher is able to use a variety of methods and tools to reach and engage students who are struggling.
The online teacher knows and understands the process for aligning teacher and student expectations for the course, in general.	The online teacher is able to orient students to teacher's instructional methods and goals and invite students to provide feedback on their perceptions of how they are learning in a course.

Standard E: The online teacher models, guides, and encourages legal, ethical, and safe behavior related to technology use.

Teacher Knowledge and Understanding	Teacher Abilities
The online teacher knows and understands the responsibilities of digital citizenship and techniques to facilitate student investigations of the legal and ethical issues related to technology and society.	The online teacher is able to establish standards for student behavior that are designed to ensure academic integrity and appropriate use of the Internet and online written communication; teach students that copyright laws are created for a reason.
The online teacher knows and understands how the use of technology may lead to instances of academic dishonesty.	The online teacher is able to identify the risks and intervene in incidents of academic dishonesty for students.
The online teacher knows and understands resources and techniques for implementing Acceptable Use Policies (AUP).	The online teacher is able to model and comply with intellectual property policies and fair use standards and reinforce their use with students.
The online teacher knows and understands techniques for recognizing and addressing the inappropriate use of electronically accessed data or information.	The online teacher is able to provide resources for students related to intellectual property and plagiarism.
The online teacher knows and understands privacy standards about other students and their posting and performance that are outlined in FERPA or other similar guidelines.	The online teacher is able to incorporate and comply with FERPA, or other similar guidelines in AUP and course design, and communicate privacy guidelines to students.

Standard F: The online teacher is cognizant of the diversity of student academic needs and incorporates accommodations into the online environment.

Teacher Knowledge and Understanding	Teacher Abilities
The online teacher knows and understands legal mandates stipulated by the Americans with Disabilities Act (ADA), the Individuals with Disabilities Education Act (IDEA), the Assistive Technology Act, and Section 508 or other similar guidelines/requirements for accessibility.	The online teacher is able to monitor student progress and apply activities and tools that are relevant to the needs of all students, including those with learning or physical disabilities, in collaboration with appropriate staff or resources.
The online teacher knows and understands that students have varied talents and skills and make appropriate accommodations designed to include all students.	The online teacher is able to address learning styles, needs for accommodations, and create multiple paths to address diverse learning styles and abilities.
The online teacher knows and understands appropriate tools and technologies to make accommodations to meet student needs.	The online teacher is able to use appropriate tools and technologies to make accommodations to meet student needs.
The online teacher knows and understands how adaptive and assistive technologies are used to help people who have disabilities gain access to information that might otherwise be inaccessible.	The online teacher is able to apply adaptive and assistive technologies in the online classroom where appropriate in the instruction to meet student needs.

(continued)

(continued)

Teacher Knowledge and Understanding	Teacher Abilities
The online teacher knows and understands options to expand student thinking, address styles of learning, and provide avenues for enrichment or intervention.	The online teacher is able to identify students who are struggling with various learning obstacles, such as ELL or literacy issues, and apply appropriate strategies to support student thinking, address styles of learning, and provide avenues for enrichment or intervention when needed.
The online teacher knows and understands the process for connecting with local support personnel to verify a student's IEP requirements or 504 accommodations needed for student success.	The online teacher is able to communicate with the appropriate school staff regarding specific accommodations, modifications, or needs as listed in a student's IEP or 504 accommodations, and work in collaboration with others to address student needs.
The online teacher knows and understands the diversity of student learning needs, languages, and backgrounds.	The online teacher is able to demonstrate awareness of different learning preferences, diversity, and universal design principles.

Standard G: The online teacher demonstrates competencies in creating and implementing assessments in online learning environments in ways that ensure validity and reliability of the instruments and procedures.

Teacher Knowledge and Understanding	Teacher Abilities
The online teacher knows and understands adequate and appropriate assessment instruments to measure online learning that reflect sufficient content validity (that is, that adequately cover the content they are designed to measure), reliability, and consistency over time.	The online teacher is able to create and implement assessments in online learning environments in ways that ensure validity and reliability of the instruments and procedures.
The online teacher knows and understands the implementation of online assessment measures and materials in ways that ensure instrument validity and reliability.	The online teacher is able to develop and deliver assessments, projects, and assignments that meet standards-based learning goals and assess learning progress by measuring student achievement of learning goals.
The online teacher knows and understands multiple strategies for ensuring the security of online student assessments, academic integrity, and assessment data.	The online teacher is able to implement a variety of assessments that ensure the security of student assessment data and accurate measures of student ability.

Standard H: The online teacher develops and delivers assessments, projects, and assignments that meet standards-based learning goals and assesses learning progress by measuring student achievement of the learning goals.

Teacher Knowledge and Understanding	Teacher Abilities
The online teacher knows and understands the reach of authentic assessments (that is, the opportunity to demonstrate understanding of acquired knowledge and skills, as opposed to testing isolated skills or retained facts) is part of the evaluation process.	The online teacher is able to apply authentic assessments as part of the evaluation process, assess student knowledge in a forum beyond traditional assessments, and monitor academic integrity with assessments.
The online teacher knows and understands the process of continuous evaluation of students to include formative and summative assessments and student feedback, including polls and surveys that reflect student learning progress throughout the course.	The online teacher is able to create or select and implement a variety of formative and summative assessments that assess student learning progress and utilize student feedback to improve the online learning experience.
The online teacher knows and understands the relationships between the assignments, assessments, and standards-based learning goals.	The online teacher is able to create, select, and organize the appropriate assignments and assessments, and align curricular content with associated and standards-based learning goals.

Standard I: The online teacher demonstrates competency in using data from assessments and other data sources to modify content and to guide student learning.

Teacher Knowledge and Understanding	Teacher Abilities
The online teacher knows and understands techniques to plan individualized instruction incorporating student data.	The online teacher is able to use student data to plan instruction.
The online teacher knows and understands how data is used to modify the content, instruction, and assessment to meet student needs.	The online teacher is able to use observational data (for example, tracking data in electronic courses, Web logs, e-mail) to monitor course progress and effectiveness.
The online teacher knows and understands how instruction is based on assessment data.	The online teacher is able to customize instruction, based on assessment data, in order to personalize the learning experience per student needs and performance.
The online teacher knows and understands the importance of self-reflection or assessment of teaching effectiveness.	The online teacher is able to create opportunities for self-reflection or assessment of teaching effectiveness within the online environment (for example, classroom assessment techniques, teacher evaluations, teacher-peer reviews).
The online teacher knows and understands varied assessment strategies that address levels of ability through a variety of alternative interventions.	The online teacher is able to address levels of ability through a variety of alternative interventions.
The online teacher knows and understands the use of effective learning strategies data for an individual student to formulate detail-specific changes in future instruction, based on assessment results and research study (data-driven and research-based).	The online teacher is able to evaluate instructional strategies to determine their accuracy and usefulness for presenting specific ideas and concepts.

(continued)

(continued)

Teacher Knowledge and Understanding	Teacher Abilities
The online teacher knows and understands the process for maintaining records of relevant communications.	
The online teacher knows and understands effective time management strategies.	The online teacher is able to provide consistent feedback and course materials in a timely manner, and use online tool functionality to improve instructional efficiency.
The online teacher knows and understands online course management tasks.	The online teacher is able to track student enrollments, communication logs, attendance records, and so on.
The online teacher knows and understands ways for teacher and students to assess student readiness for course content and method of delivery.	The online teacher is able to employ ways to assess student readiness for course content and method of delivery.
The online teacher knows and understands that student success (for example, grade, level of participation, mastery of content, completion percentage) is an important measure of teaching and course success.	The online teacher is able to employ ways for students to effectively evaluate and assess their own readiness for course content and method of delivery.
The online teacher knows and understands the importance of student self-assessment.	The online teacher is able to create opportunities for student self-assessment within courses.
The online teacher knows and understands the role of student empowerment in online learning.	The online teacher is able to empower students to independently define short- and long-term learning goals and monitor their personal progress.

Standard J: The online teacher interacts in a professional, effective manner with colleagues, parents, and other members of the community to support students' success.

Teacher Knowledge and Understanding	Teacher Abilities
The online teacher knows and understands the need for professional activity and collaboration beyond school (for example, professional learning communities) to update academic skills and knowledge and collaborate with other educators.	The online teacher is able to engage in professional development activities and collaboration beyond school.
The online teacher knows and understands the need to coordinate learning experiences with other adults involved in providing support to the student (for example, parents, local school contacts, mentors) to support student learning.	The online teacher is able to provide ongoing communication with parents or guardians concerning student learning.

Standard K (for teachers involved in instructional design): The online teacher arranges media and content to help students and teachers transfer knowledge most effectively in the online environment.

Teacher Knowledge and Understanding

- The online teacher knows and understands critical digital literacies and twenty-first century skills. The online teacher knows and understands appropriate use of technologies to enhance learning.

Teacher Abilities

- The online teacher is able to modify and add content and assessment, using an online learning management system (LMS).

- The online teacher is able to create and modify engaging content and appropriate assessments in an online environment.

- The online teacher is able to incorporate multimedia and visual resources into an online module.

- The online teacher is able to use and incorporate subject-specific and developmentally appropriate software in an online learning module.

- The online teacher is able to review materials and Web resources for their alignment with course objectives and state and local standards and for their appropriateness on a continuing basis.

- The online teacher is able to create assignments, projects, and assessments that are aligned with students' different visual, auditory, and hands-on ways of learning.

- The online teacher is able to arrange media and content to help transfer knowledge most effectively in the online environment.

FREQUENTLY ASKED QUESTIONS

In many ways, online learning is disrupting the world of education. More and more students are coming to online learning looking for something completely different. They've been disillusioned by the traditional system and know there must be a better way. In many ways, online learning is meeting those needs.

Although we know that online education is taking the world by storm and a growing option in many areas, the general public still knows very little about online learning. They don't understand how someone could learn at a distance and they understand even less about how a teacher might be involved in that system. At the beginning of this revolution, part of your job will be to act as an educator and an evangelist for the public.

You'll also find yourself talking to other teachers quite a bit and explaining your work to them. They're feeling the pressure to move more toward online learning and that can be scary! For teachers, you'll need to allay their fears and help them understand that online learning is still "real" school and an exciting way to work!

The following are just samplings of the questions you may receive when you tell people that you're an online teacher as well as some basic ways to answer those questions well.

So, wait, how does online teaching work? Do you spend all day on a webcam?

No, we have a learning management system in which kids are getting what they need to complete my course. Sometimes I might be on a webcam helping my students but most of the time we're working in that system at different times. I'm creating course content, answering questions, and grading assignments while they're working through the content I create for them. I help set the pace for the course but they have a lot of flexibility in where and how they learn.

Don't you miss the kids?

The kinds of interactions that I have with kids in an online course are different than the ones I have in a traditional course. However, there's still a lot of interaction. I'm not just talking to a screen all day. I'm talking to real kids with real lives and real concerns. I just happen to talk to them through a screen instead of face-to-face. Even so, there's actually a lot of interaction that happens in an online class. We're posting to a discussion board, e-mailing, chatting, and even talking on the phone. I'm posting announcements, sending grades and feedback, and facilitating on the discussion board. I am not at all isolated. In fact, I'm even more connected to kids than I was as a traditional teacher.

How do you know that students aren't cheating?

A lot of that goes into the design of the course. The courses have to be designed in such a way that they are not easily ''Googleable.'' Students are creating projects, designing new products, and so on that they can't just find on the Internet. It also comes down to the teacher. Teachers in an online course need to have a good feel for their student's abilities. If something unusual happens, it's the teacher's job to contact the student and see what's up. Beyond that, there are all sorts of online checks and balances to prevent cheating, including online plagiarism detectors that compare written assignments to content on the entire World Wide Web to ensure that the work is original.

In the end, however, we have to eventually trust the student. Most students, when they're genuinely asked, realize that they need to learn these things to succeed in the real world. They generally cheat when they don't have the time to do the work or the pressure is too great. In an average circumstance, students will do the work if they see it as valuable. It's my job to make sure they do!

What do *you* do as an online teacher?

My job is quite a bit different from that of a face-to-face teacher because in most online courses the curriculum and materials are already written. Instead of spending a lot of time planning new lessons, I'm spending most of my time monitoring the course and providing feedback. Primarily, my job falls into three main categories:

Preparing: I have to ensure that upcoming assignments are clear, due dates are visible, and students have an understanding of what's coming up. I change the course materials or add supplemental materials when it will deepen the learning.

Monitoring: I have to be a part of the discussion boards on a regular basis. I read every post. I add posts that will deepen the learning and send us off in new directions. I am a learner in the course along with the students and I ensure that my presence is public to them. I have to know how much time each student is spending in the course and when students are falling behind. I am a constant presence. I monitor everything that's happening there.

Feedback: Students don't have the benefit of nonverbal feedback in an online course so a good part of my work is providing students with in-depth feedback. Assignments are graded within forty-eight hours most of the time. Each assignment has written feedback from me. Students who are doing well receive an e-mail with kudos on their progress. Those who need a little prodding also get an e-mail or a text. They know I'm watching and that I care. I will push them on to the next level.

There's so much learning that happens in a classroom that's not part of the syllabus. Don't the students miss out?

There's a lot that happens outside the syllabus in an online course, too. First, in the area of information. Because of the flexibility of the Internet and hyperlinks, online courses have significant depth. Students can immediately link to find more information about their topic. Once a student becomes familiar with online learning, this becomes a regular, welcome part of their learning experience.

Second, in the area of interaction. Students interact with each other through discussion boards and interactive projects. Because discussions on the boards are graded, quiet students aren't allowed to sit back and listen. They have to be an active part of the class, too. Thankfully, the online medium gives them a chance to respond in a completely new way. The introverted student can read posts, draft a response, and proofread before ever speaking out. It allows for a kind of reflection that's just not possible face-to-face. These discussions have far more depth and breadth than what you might find in a traditional classroom.

Finally, in the area of distribution. Students in my online course are creating these amazing products in the form of wikis, blogs, and even movies that just aren't possible in a traditional classroom. Not only that, but once they complete a project, their audience can be the entire world instead of just their teacher. That's a really powerful way to learn!

What kinds of students are in an online class?

They vary a lot! Some are kids that just didn't fit in a traditional setting. Some are taking courses that aren't available at their local school. Some just want the experience of online learning. Some are working three grade levels ahead. Some are three grade levels behind. The beauty of online learning is that it's anonymous. All these kids can work together in the same classroom without any of the usual stigma. That anonymity allows for much deeper learning.

Who writes the courses? Can you change things?

Usually online teachers are teaching courses they didn't write. In most organizations, all online courses are reviewed on a regular basis and updated to meet standards of online learning (iNACOL has a set of good standards). Whether or not the courses can be updated depends on the organization you're working for. Some allow you to change anything. Some allow you to change nothing. Some allow you to add but not delete. It all depends on the school. For me, I like to change my courses regularly and update them for students' needs. It's one of the most exciting parts of the work.

Aren't you afraid you'll be replaced by a computer?

Absolutely not! Good online learning will always have a good teacher behind the wheel. Programs that are successful still have caring teachers consistently working with students and challenging them to do their personal best. Those teachers are just connecting via a computer instead of face-to-face. That will continue to be the case in the future and good teachers will always have jobs.

Although these are the basic questions you'll get, there will always be curious, maybe even doubtful, people with all sorts of questions about what you do. Your best option is to stay positive and share your story. People will be impressed by your enthusiasm for students and for the way you work!

REFERENCES

Anderson, T. (2008). Toward a theory of online learning. In T. Anderson (Ed.), *The theory and practice of online learning* (2nd ed., pp. 33–60). Edmonton, Canada: Athabasca University Press.

Christensen, C. M., Horn, M. B., & Johnson, C. W. (2009). *Disrupting class: How disruptive innovation will change the way the world learns.* New York: McGraw-Hill Professional.

Gabriel, T. (2011, April 5). More pupils are learning online, fueling debate on quality. *New York Times.* Retrieved from www.nytimes.com/2011/04/06/education/06online.html?pagewanted=all&_r=0

Horn, M. B., & Staker, H. (2011). *The rise of K–12 blended learning.* San Mateo, CA: Innosight Institute.

International Association for K–12 Online Learning. (2011). *iNACOL national standards for quality online courses, version 2.* Retrieved from www.inacol.org/research/nationalstandards/iNACOL_CourseStandards_2011.pdf

Lenhart, A., Ling, R., Campbell, S., & Purcell, K. (2010, April 20). *Teens and mobile phones: Social network sites, face-to-face meetings, landline calls, instant messaging, and email.* Pew Internet Research. Retrieved from http://pewinternet.org/Reports/2010/Teens-and-Mobile-Phones/Chapter-2/Other-methods.aspx

Nielsen Wire. (2010). *U.S. teen mobile report: Calling yesterday, texting today, using apps tomorrow.* Retrieved from http://blog.nielsen.com/nielsenwire/online_mobile/u-s-teen-mobile-report-calling-yesterday-texting-today-using-apps-tomorrow/

Saul, S. (2011, December 12). Profits and questions at online charter schools. *New York Times.* Retrieved from www.nytimes.com/2011/12/13/education/online-schools-score-better-on-wall-street-than-in-classrooms.html?pagewanted=all

Savery, J. (2005). Be VOCAL: Characteristics of successful online instructors. *Journal of Interactive Online Learning, 4*(2), 141–152.

US Department of Education. (2010, September). *Evaluation of evidence-based practices in online learning: A meta-analysis and review of online learning studies.* Retrieved from www2.ed.gov/rschstat/eval/tech/evidence-based-practices/finalreport.pdf

Wyatt, K., & Moreno, I. (2011, December 16). Virtual schools booming as states mull warnings. *Huffington Post.* Retrieved from www.huffingtonpost.com/2011/12/16/virtual-schools-booming-a_0_n_1154261.html

RESOURCES

When I first began teaching online, I did what any good teacher might do. I started searching for professional development books! I wanted to know what other teachers were doing and what they said about how to do this work well. Unfortunately I didn't find a lot out there. At the time, online learning for secondary students was fairly new and there were very few, if any, good resources for how to do the work. Although online learning is still a relatively recent addition, there are starting to be more and more good resources for finding out how to do the work well.

INACOL — AN EXCELLENT PROFESSIONAL ORGANIZATION

One of the best resources out there for learning more about online teaching is the International Association for K–12 Online Learning (iNACOL). They're a professional organization focused on advocacy and education in the area of online teaching and learning in the K–12 classroom. As online learning has spread throughout the country, iNACOL has been leading the way and growing along with it.

On iNACOL's website, you'll find an amazing collection of resources including their Promising Practices series. Promising Practices highlights the findings of researchers into what works in an online classroom. Issues such as socialization and blended learning have been highlighted recently and iNACOL shares some great ideas about how to improve. iNACOL also publishes a yearly collection of the latest research about what's working in online and blended learning classrooms. In addition to these print resources, iNACOL also sponsors monthly webinars for teachers. The guest speakers are excellent, knowledgeable professionals in the field and can really shed light on what works. Although there is a fee for attending a webinar live, these webinars are all recorded and shared in the iNACOL forums for viewing by any member, free of charge.

If you decide to purchase a membership in iNACOL, you'll also want to check out their forums. Their online forums are a great way to connect with other professionals. Although the forums aren't all that active, each board provides the option to subscribe and receive an e-mail when there are new posts. I've found that I receive lots of responses when I post questions because members get those e-mails and can visit the boards to answer. The job board is particularly active and can be a great way to find job postings!

VIRTUAL SCHOOL SYMPOSIUM – KNOWING YOU'RE NOT ALONE

In addition to iNACOL's online resources, they also host a yearly conference called the Virtual School Symposium (VSS). The 2011 conference had more than two thousand attendees, with breakout sessions on everything from starting online programs to working with at-risk learners. VSS is a really valuable experience that's well worth the money to attend. In addition to all the breakout sessions, you'll get to meet lots of other online teachers and pick their brains about what works. It's a great way to network and reaffirm that you're not alone in this business!

DEVELOPING A PERSONAL LEARNING NETWORK

Finally, you'll want to spend some time creating a personal learning network (PLN). A PLN is a collection of blogs, discussion boards, and Twitter feeds that you can read regularly to expand your thinking. There are some amazing educators out there and, through the power of the Internet, you can tap into the best of the best. Spending some time each day on Google Reader can be a fantastic way to connect to new ideas and invigorate your practice.

Then, as you gain experience, you can become an active participant, too. Through posting your ideas on a blog or Twitter feed, you'll expand your own thinking as well as find new people to follow. Social media has made all sorts of deeper learning possible for educators, especially online educators.

Following are some suggestions for blogs and Twitter feeds you may want to start with. Have fun!

RECOMMENDED BLOGS

- Education Frontier, found at http://Educationfrontier.org
  - This is my blog and the companion to this book. I first started blogging in 2007 as a way to process what I was learning about online teaching. I try to be very real on the blog, sharing frustrations as well as new ideas.

- Virtual High School Meanderings, found at http://virtualschooling .wordpress.com
  - This is a very active blog that gathers tidbits about online learning from across the web. It can be a great way to stay on top of media coverage of the field.

- Susan Patrick iNACOL blog, found at http://susanpatrick.inacol.org
  - Susan Patrick, head of iNACOL, has recently started a blog with tidbits about online learning and iNACOL. Her posts about what staff are reading at iNACOL that week are a fascinating collection of the latest in online learning.

- The Fischbowl, found at http://thefischbowl.blogspot.com
  - Karl Fisch is an educator in Colorado. Although his blog is not specifically about online education, he has a lot to say about educational technology. You'll find his ideas thought-provoking.

Note: You may want to investigate a tool like Google Reader or Feed Demon to compile all your blogs into one space. By simply subscribing to the RSS feed of a particular blog, all new posts will appear in your RSS reader. It makes following your favorite blogs a lot easier!

RECOMMENDED TWITTER FEEDS

- @educationweek
  - This is the Twitter feed for the *Education Week* publication. They're constantly sharing blog posts and interesting articles as food for thought.

- @NewTechNetwork
  - This is a group of schools focused on learning with technology through Project Based Learning. There's a lot of potential for project-based learning in the online classroom and this organization is leading the way.

- @iNACOL
  - iNACOL is using social media more and more to connect with its members and its Twitter feed is used in addition to Facebook and its blog.

- @EdFrontier
  - This is my Twitter feed. I try to post only items that are specifically relevant to online education and education reform.

- Other interesting Twitter feeds to consider:
  - @mwacker
  - @tvanderark
  - @Bruce_Friend
  - @CarriSchneider

TWITTER HASHTAGS RELATED TO ONLINE LEARNING

Although hashtags can change all the time on Twitter, having a basic set to start with can help you find new people to follow very quickly. Here are a few basics:

#edu

#onlineed

#vss__ (posts from the Virtual School Symposium—insert correct year)

#iste (posts related to the International Society for Technology in Education)

#edchat (collection of ideas about change in education)

#pblchat (weekly chat about project-based learning)

#inacol

TRAINING COURSES ON HOW TO BECOME AN ONLINE TEACHER

More and more programs are starting to offer courses on how to become an online teacher. The following are worth exploring more:

- PBS Teacherline: "Online Facilitation Strategies I"
  - This course provides a basic overview of the skills and strategies required to become an online teacher. They employ an excellent model of online education and demonstrate how to use it effectively in this course.
    - www.pbs.org/teacherline/catalog/courses/TECH522/
- Ed Tech Leaders Online (ETLO)
  - ETLO provides a series of courses on how to be an online facilitator, from designing online courses to advanced facilitation strategies
    - http://edtechleaders.org/

BOOKS FOR ONLINE TEACHERS

Although most of the resources that are out there for online teachers are focused on the postsecondary market, there are still some excellent texts out there that are worth considering, even if you do have to adjust the strategies for the grade level you teach. Here are a few:

- Jossey-Bass has published a series of books about online teaching. Some of the titles include *Engaging the Online Learner, Managing Online Instructor*

Workload, and *Assessing the Online Learner*. The strategies are focused on the postsecondary classroom but many of them are excellent and could easily be modified for a fifth- through twelfth-grade classroom.

- *The Online Teaching Survival Guide: Simple and Practical Pedagogical Tips* by Judith Boettcher is also worth your consideration. Boettcher says that it's best to divide the online course into four phases. In each phase, the instructor needs to focus on different tasks. In the first phase, the teacher's primary focus is on supporting and getting to know students. Then, through each of the other three phases the teacher gradually releases responsibility so that by the end of the course, the students are working in small groups and presenting content, many times independently.

These resources are a great place to start but there are new resources out there daily. It's exciting to be a part of this growing community!

GLOSSARY

Blended (or hybrid) learning Occurs when a course has elements of a physical classroom blended with elements of an online classroom. Students spend some time face-to-face with the teacher but also spend some time working in an online setting.

Discussion board A space in an LMS where students can have a written discussion about a particular topic. Students can easily respond to each other's ideas. Also called *forum* or *threaded discussion*.

Learning management system (LMS) The space where you teach your online course. It will have basic tools such as a discussion board, grade book, and a place to share content. This is usually the home base for your online courses. Blackboard, Schoology, Desire2Learn, and Moodle are common LMS examples.

Master course The starting copy of a course for any given semester. All copies of the course are created from this one master course. Although teachers will make modifications to their copy of the course throughout the year, they usually come back to the original master course when a new year begins to maintain course consistency.

Podcast An audio recording that can be downloaded to a media player. Podcasts can be used to share content with students. They can be just a teacher's voice or a combination of voice and music. Possible content includes interviews, lectures on content, or student-created items. The video version of a podcast is called a *vodcast*.

Screencast A video that shows your screen in real time with a voiceover. Jing and Screencast are common tools for this purpose.

Synchronous Elements of a synchronous course are happening at the same time. A webinar is the most commonly found synchronous element in a course, when everyone in the class is getting on at the same time to have a discussion about the course content.

Vodcast A video version of a *podcast*.

Voiceboard An online discussion board that allows students to add their recorded voice comments instead of just communicating in text. This tool is a great way to expose students to public speaking opportunities in a digital space. Voicethread is an example tool but many LMSs also have these features integrated into their systems.

Web 2.0 tools Tools students can use on the Internet to create and share content.

Webinar A synchronous session within a course in which students can get together in real time with the teacher and discuss course content. Chat, audio, video, screen sharing, and record tools are common features.

Wiki A website that is very easy for multiple people to edit. Often used in online courses for group projects.

Zero week The first week of an online course when students are introducing themselves to the class and getting familiar with the tools of the online classroom. Called a *zero week* because there's very little if any course content during the first sessions while students are getting oriented to the online tools.

ACKNOWLEDGMENTS

I'd like to extend my heartfelt thanks to all the wonderful people and organizations that have helped to make this book possible. First, to my husband, Daniel Kipp, who has encouraged me every step of the way and put up with long hours of discussing online learning. Next, to my employer Jefferson County Schools, which has created a wonderful working environment in which I can experiment, innovate, and find new ways of reaching students in the online classroom. Next, thanks to the sponsors of the National Online Teacher of the Year award, especially the International Association for K–12 Online Learning (iNACOL) and the Southern Regional Education Board (SREB), who gave me a voice and showed me that teachers' opinions can make a difference in the lives of students across the country. And finally, my sincere thanks to Diane Kornegay, assistant superintendent for instruction in Clay County, Florida, who first encouraged me to write a book and persisted in her encouragement when I tried to laugh off the idea. I appreciate the nudge!

INDEX